Penn State

State College, Pennsylvania

Written by Alyssa Fried and Tim Williams

Edited by Adam Burns, Jon Skindzier, and Meryl Sustarsic

Layout by Kimberly Moore

Additional contributions by Omid Gohari, Christina Koshzow, Chris Mason, Joey Rahimi, and Luke Skurman

ISBN # 1-4247-0109-8
© Copyright 2006 College Prowler
All Rights Reserved
Printed in the U.S.A.
www.collegeprowler.com

Last updated 5/16/06

Special Thanks To: Babs Carryer, Andy Hannah, LaunchCyte, Tim O'Brien, Bob Sehlinger, Thomas Emerson, Andrew Skurman, Barbara Skurman, Bert Mann, Dave Lehman, Daniel Fayock, Chris Babyak, The Donald H. Jones Center for Entrepreneurship, Terry Slease, Jerry McGinnis, Bill Ecenberger, Idie McGinty, Kyle Russell, Jacque Zaremba, Larry Winderbaum, Roland Allen, Jon Reider, Team Evankovich, Lauren Varacalli, Abu Noaman, Mark Exler, Daniel Steinmeyer, Jared Cohon, Gabriela Oates, David Koegler, Glen Meakem, and the Penn State Bounce-Back Team.

College Prowler®
5001 Baum Blvd.
Suite 750
Pittsburgh, PA 15213

Phone: 1-800-290-2682
Fax: 1-800-772-4972
E-Mail: info@collegeprowler.com
Web Site: www.collegeprowler.com

Welcome to College Prowler®

During the writing of College Prowler's guidebooks, we felt it was critical that our content was unbiased and unaffiliated with any college or university. We think it's important that our readers get honest information and a realistic impression of the student opinions on any campus—that's why if any aspect of a particular school is terrible, we (unlike a campus brochure) intend to publish it. While we do keep an eye out for the occasional extremist—the cheerleader or the cynic—we take pride in letting the students tell it like it is. We strive to create a book that's as representative as possible of each particular campus. Our books cover both the good and the bad, and whether the survey responses point to recurring trends or a variation in opinion, these sentiments are directly and proportionally expressed through our guides.

College Prowler guidebooks are in the hands of students throughout the entire process of their creation. Because you can't make student-written guides without the students, we have students at each campus who help write, randomly survey their peers, edit, layout, and perform accuracy checks on every book that we publish. From the very beginning, student writers gather the most up-to-date stats, facts, and inside information on their colleges. They fill each section with student quotes and summarize the findings in editorial reviews. In addition, each school receives a collection of letter grades (A through F) that reflect student opinion and help to represent contentment, prominence, or satisfaction for each of our 20 specific categories. Just as in grade school, the higher the mark the more content, more prominent, or more satisfied the students are with the particular category.

Once a book is written, additional students serve as editors and check for accuracy even more extensively. Our bounce-back team—a group of randomly selected students who have no involvement with the project—are asked to read over the material in order to help ensure that the book accurately expresses every aspect of the university and its students. This same process is applied to the 200-plus schools College Prowler currently covers. Each book is the result of endless student contributions, hundreds of pages of research and writing, and countless hours of hard work. All of this has led to the creation of a student information network that stretches across the nation to every school that we cover. It's no easy accomplishment, but it's the reason that our guides are such a great resource.

When reading our books and looking at our grades, keep in mind that every college is different and that the students who make up each school are not uniform—as a result, it is important to assess schools on a case-by-case basis. Because it's impossible to summarize an entire school with a single number or description, each book provides a dialogue, not a decision, that's made up of 20 different topics and hundreds of student quotes. In the end, we hope that this guide will serve as a valuable tool in your college selection process. Enjoy!

OMID GOHARI ◯ CHRISTINA KOSHZOW ◯ CHRIS MASON ◯ JOEY RAHIMI ◯ LUKE SKURMAN ◯
The College Prowler Team

Table of Contents

Introduction from the Author

In 2005, Penn State celebrated its 150th birthday. Since it opened as an agricultural school on a large mass of vacant land in 1855, PSU has become one of the largest universities in the country, encompassing 11 campuses and over 90,000 students and faculty. It is also among the leading research institutions in the nation, and has made important and often historical breakthroughs in every field, from the study of American literature to nuclear science.

Of course, you cannot mention Penn State in conversation without mentioning the famous Nittany Lion football team or Joe Paterno, the most successful college football coach of all time. Both the team and its leader serve as the ultimate example of Penn State pride!

For all its accomplishments and continuous growth, Penn State remains a learning institution. Higher-level courses are kept small, teacher to student ratios are low, and student academics are a priority. Every effort is made to keep students from feeling "lost in the crowd" at such an enormous school.

When I first came to Penn State, I was undecided about my major. I knew it was somewhere between English, art history and conservation, photography, and telecommunications; or perhaps it was something I hadn't yet discovered. Penn State was one of few schools in the East to offer great programs for each of my prospective majors and many others I might have considered. I also received a taste of what it meant to be part of the Penn State community. It seems as though every person I meet, even outside of campus, has a connection to the school.

This book is intended to give you, the reader, a fair and unbiased view of all that Penn State has to offer, as well as what it may be lacking. Hopefully, it'll help make the most difficult decision you've faced in 18 years a little easier.

Alyssa Fried, Author
Penn State University

By the Numbers

General Information

Penn State
201 Old Main
State College, PA 16802

Control:
Public

Academic Calendar:
Semester

Religious Affiliation:
None

Founded:
1855

Web Site:
www.psu.edu

Main Phone:
(814) 865-4700

Admissions Phone:
(814) 865-5471

Student Body

**Full-Time
Undergraduates:**
33,376

**Part-Time
Undergraduates:**
1,448

**Total Male
Undergraduates:**
18,663

**Total Female
Undergraduates:**
16,161

Admissions

Overall Acceptance Rate:
58%

Total Applicants:
30,122

Total Acceptances:
17,551

Freshman Enrollment:
5,907

Yield (% of admitted students who actually enroll):
35%

Early Decision Available?
No

Early Action Available?
No

Regular Decision Deadline:
Rolling

Regular Decision Notification:
Rolling

Must-Reply-By Date:
May 1

Transfer Applications Received:
1,303

Transfer Applications Accepted:
614

Transfer Students Enrolled:
362

Common Application Accepted?
None

Supplemental Forms?
None

Admissions E-Mail:
admissions@psu.edu

Admissions Web Site:
www.psu.edu/dept/admissions

SAT I or ACT Required?
Either

First-Year Students Submitting SAT Scores:
97%

SAT I Range (25th–75th Percentile):
1090–1300

SAT I Verbal Range (25th–75th Percentile):
530–630

SAT I Math Range (25th–75th Percentile):
560–670

Retention Rate:
93%

Top 10% of High School Class:
43%

Application Fee:
$50

Financial Information

In-State Tuition:
$9,822

Out-of-State Tuition:
$19,732

Average Need-Based Financial Aid Package (including loans, work-study, grants, and other sources):
$13,602

Students Who Applied for Financial Aid:
66%

Students Who Received Aid:
50%

Financial Aid Forms Deadline:
February 15

Financial Aid Phone:
(814) 865-6301

Financial Aid E-Mail:
www.work.psu.edu/dept/ studentaid/email/email.html

Financial Aid Web Site:
www.psu.edu/dept/ studentaid

Academics

The Lowdown On...
Academics

Degrees Awarded:
Bachelor
Master
Doctorate

Most Popular Majors:
21% Business/Marketing
13% Engineering
9% Communications
7% Education
9% Social Sciences

Full-Time Faculty:
2,143

Faculty with Terminal Degree:
77%

Student-to-Faculty Ratio:
18:1

Undergraduate Schools:

The College of Agricultural Sciences

The College of Arts and Architecture

The College of Communications

The College of Earth and Mineral Sciences

The College of Education

The College of Engineering

The College of Health and Human Development

The College of Liberal Arts

The Eberly College of Science

The School of Information Sciences and Technology

The Smeal College of Business Administration

Graduation Rates:

Four-Year: 48%

Five-Year: 79%

Six-Year: 82%

AP Test Score Requirements

Accepted AP test scores range from 3 to 5. For a detailed listing, visit *www.psu.edu/admissions/requirements/firstyear/ap.htm*

IB Test Score Requirements

Accepted IB test scores are 5 or higher. For more information, visit *www.psu.edu/admissions/requirements/firstyear/ib.htm*

Academic Clubs

There are 168 academic Clubs on campus ranging from the Accounting Club to Xi Sigma Pi. For a full listing, check out *www.sa.psu.edu/usa/studentactivities/UserMain.asp*

Did You Know?

Thirty percent of classes have **fewer than 20 students**.

There are **415 registered organizations** and 65 honor societies on campus.

Best Places to Study

The Library, dorm study lounges, the Hub

Students Speak Out On...
Academics

"You'll have helpful, interesting professors, and you'll also have know-it-all, uninvolved professors. The majority of classes are large, so it's hard to get to a one-on-one basis with the professors."

Q "**The teachers are friendly** but won't pay much attention to you personally unless you approach them first. It's very hard to meet with teachers because they have a very busy schedule."

Q "**The teachers are very easy to approach** because they don't get a lot of one-to-one, student-teacher action. Professors lecture most classes, but the day-to-day questions and problems are handled by teaching assistants (TAs) and grad students. The exams are also almost exclusively proctored by TAs and grad students."

Q "The teachers at Penn State are, for the most part, really cool. **Everyone here likes the sociology classes** because those classes have the coolest teachers. There's work involved with all classes, but look for classes that allow discussions and debates."

Q "I think the teachers are good here. They know what they are talking about, but **you do run into the huge lecture classes**. Some TAs barely speak English, but I hear that happens elsewhere, too."

Q **"I have had great experiences with my professors**; they're all very accommodating and understanding. But I have to caution you that general education classes— the classes that you have to take to be a 'well-balanced' student—will be crowded. In order to fulfill a requirement, I took an introduction with 232 students that was held in a big auditorium. In the classes I take for my major, I don't have a single class where there were more than 44 other students in it. The labs usually have between 15–25 students."

Q "The teachers I had were all pretty great. I took lots of interesting classes I never would have imagined would be available and so exciting. **There are lots of great theater classes, too.**"

Q "**School is pretty challenging.** Depending on how well you can retain information, whether you like to go to class or not, and your study habits, it's not impossible to receive an 'A' here. But with all the distractions around, it's almost impossible to stay ahead and not cram on occasion."

Q "The downside of academics here is the professor/student relationship, or the lack thereof. Neither one cares about the other, nor even gets to know your name. **Most of my classes are small**, but some of the business classes can be as many as 600 students for one professor."

Q "The teachers are like prizes in Cracker Jack boxes: some are cool and worth trying for, while others simply suck. Some are here to do research and that's all they care about, so their classes put you to sleep faster than NyQuil. The teachers who are here for the students are the ones who rock, and **their classes are actually fun to attend.**"

Q "**Professors really run the gamut.** Usually you will be stuck with several TAs before you come across a REAL professor with real-life hair and beard and a kung fu grip. It is usually when you get into upper-level courses that you become really acquainted with one or two professors."

The College Prowler Take On...
Academics

From the foreign grad student who barely speaks English to the wise old department head who practically invented your major, all kinds of instructors can be found lecturing in the classrooms and auditoriums at Penn State. The majority of the professors are middle-aged and quite accomplished in their fields. Many of the teachers are there because they want to be, but there is, of course, a minority of professors who are more interested in their own research than instructing students.

Class size also varies widely. It's easy to get lost in the large auditorium classes, but these are unavoidable when you're working on general requirements. As you progress in a major, though, you'll find that classes become smaller, more discussion-oriented, and more personal. Penn State has a lot to offer academically, and this is especially true if you're motivated to learn.

B

The College Prowler® Grade on
Academics: B

A high Academics grade generally indicates that professors are knowledgeable, accessible, and genuinely interested in their students' welfare. Other determining factors include class size, how well professors communicate, and whether or not classes are engaging.

Local Atmosphere

The Lowdown On...
Local Atmosphere

Region:
Middle Atlantic

City, State:
State College, PA

Setting:
College town

Distance from Philadelphia:
3 hours, 30 minutes

Distance from Pittsburgh:
3 hours

Points of Interest:
Mount Nittany
(Hiking, Biking)

Museum of Fine Arts

Penn Roosevelt State Park
(Camping, Fishing)

Tussey Mountain
(Skiing, Skating)

➔

Closest Shopping Malls:

Nittany Mall

Closest Movie Theaters:

Carmike Cinema 5
116 Heister St., State College
(814) 237-7657

Carmike Cinema 6
501 Benner Pike, (across from
the Nittany Mall)
(814) 237-1997

Garman Opera House
116 East High St., Bellefonte
(814) 353-8803

Major Sports Teams:

Penn State Nittany Lions
(Football)

Lady Lions (Basketball)

City Web Sites

www.statecollege.com
www.happyvalley.com

Did You Know?

5 Fun Facts about State College

- Each year downtown State College hosts the Central Pennsylvania Festival of the Arts, **a huge sidewalk sale and exhibition** that draws artisans from across the country and brings in over 100,000 visitors!

- The **Centre County Grange Fair**, held annually outside of State College, is one of the largest and last-remaining tenting fairs in the world.

- Penn State's Beaver Stadium is the **Second largest stadium in the United States**, with 106,537 seats.

- *Psychology Today* **ranked State College Number One** as the lowest stress city in the United States.

- "**Nittany**" is a Native American term meaning "single mountain."

Students Speak Out On...
Local Atmosphere

> "State College is a relaxing, friendly, college town that can make anyone feel at home. There isn't much to visit, though, since we really are in the middle of nowhere."

Q "State College is purely a Penn State town. While the residents may complain a lot about the students, their economy would be down the drain if it wasn't for the University. The **University and its students play a major role** in the town."

Q "The town is basically an off-shoot of the University. Residents here feed off of us kids and complain about it the whole time. Basically, **Penn State 'owns' State College** and the townies would be nothing without 40,000 students. In terms of places to visit, besides Beaver Stadium there are just a bunch of state parks."

Q "State College is definitely a college town. The majority of the town is geared towards the students. However, most of the town consists of bars. **The University does offer quite a bit of underage activities**, including free movies, billiards, and ping pong."

Q "The town is great. Everyone is there for Penn State. **There is a lot of pride in being a Nittany Lion**. There are tons of stores selling just PSU stuff. On the down side, University Park is in the middle of nowhere. Pittsburgh and Philly are both about three hours away; New York City is about five."

Q "If you're keen on drinking, there are **more than enough bars** to suit your fancy. There's also a little bit of shopping to do, although most of it is Penn State apparel, unfortunately."

Q "**I like the atmosphere PSU offers**. The campus holds all kinds of activities for the students (movies, games, athletics, and art), while off-campus activities (chillin' with friends, bar-hopping, camping, and fishing) give everyone a chance to free themselves from feeling like a student all the time. No other universities are even around State College."

Q "During the academic year, the town is full of students who are out for a good evening. It gets busy on the nicer weekends. **There are plenty of shops**, families, and hippies. During the summer, the town is full of townies and the only thing to do is drink, hike Mt. Nittany, visit Bellefonte, and make trips to Denny's."

Q "It's entirely a college town, dominated by the University. **The atmosphere is laid-back** and that of a society run by 20-somethings and 20-somethings alone. It's kind of like *Lord of the Flies*, but with booze. Don't leave town alone, especially if you are going to interact with locals. Otherwise, it's worth a visit to Bellefonte, the drive-in theater, and Penn's Cave."

Q "There are no other universities in the area that I know of, unless you count the Altoona campus, which is a forty minute drive away. The atmosphere as a whole is very nice. **The campus is very well-taken care of**, and is a nice place to live. Downtown State College is a generally nice area, but it could use a bit of sprucing up to match the quality of the campus. Landlords and business owners seem a bit too eager to put in the money to develop new areas away from campus rather than to maintain the downtown area."

The College Prowler Take On...
Local Atmosphere

The town of State College has been fairly judged as a party town. The town's population and activity level rises and falls with the academic calendar. During the day, downtown State College is a decent shopping ground for any 15–25-year-old. The area surrounding State College is almost always undergoing development, with new shopping plazas, restaurants, and movie theaters being added every year. This part of town is more accessible if you have a car, though there is a public transportation system if you're willing to keep to its erratic schedule.

At night, the stores close and the bars open. It's easy to find a party, but if you don't want to drink or party you may be left out in the cold. Remember, if you choose to live here, that State College is the only sizable town for over a hundred miles. Other universities are only present during athletic competitions. A good season for the Nittany Lion's football team makes for a happy populace.

The College Prowler® Grade on
Local
Atmosphere: C+

A high Local Atmosphere grade indicates that the area surrounding campus is safe and scenic. Other factors include nearby attractions, proximity to other schools, and the town's attitude toward students.

Safety & Security

The Lowdown On...
Safety & Security

Number of PSU Police:
53

Number of PSU Security Staff:
250

PSU Police Phone:
(814) 863-1111

Safety Services:
Escort Service: (814) 865-WALK
Emergency Phones

Health Services:
Alcohol Intervention
Contraception Counseling
Emergency Medical Services
Health Education Services
HIV Testing and Counseling
Nutrition Clinic
Pharmacy
Tobacco Cessation Counseling

Health Center Web Site:
www.sa.psu.edu/uhs

Health Center Office Hours

Monday–Friday 8 a.m.–5 p.m.
Saturday (urgent care) 11 a.m.–3 p.m.

Did You Know?

The police officers at University Park campus:

- Have a **bachelor's degree in social services**.
- Have **completed the training course** required of all municipal police officers in PA.
- Take **90 to 100 hours** of in-service training each year.

> "I have never had any safety problems on campus. There were a few incidents of people breaking into dorms, but I never knew any victims."

Q "**The dorm buildings are controlled by key card access**. It is up to the student, however, to keep their individual dorm room locked. A few attacks have occurred from students leaving their rooms unlocked. There are blue-light security phones all over campus, and an escort service can walk you home at all hours of the night if you feel you need it."

Q "**There is a free escort security service** provided by the campus if you are out downtown or even across campus late at night. Overall though, State College is a very safe and friendly town."

Q "**I feel very safe**. There aren't as many blue lights here compared to other campuses I've been to, but I feel safe walking around at 4 a.m. on weekdays or weekends. There's a campus security escort group, and if you call them, they'll walk you home. I must mention, however, the year before I attended, there was some hate mail sent to an African American group. I still feel safe there, though."

Q "**Security is good here—almost too good**. There's a ton of employees in the campus police force that like to show you how important they are. They hold shifts 24/7 to make sure we can all sleep at night.

Q "Late at night, the campus is very dark. If you want, **you can call the escort service**. They walk or drive students home if needed."

Q "**Carry a mobile phone** on you if you are remotely concerned for your safety, although crime in State College is more or less non-existent."

Q "Security and safety are great here. They don't seem to skimp on it. If you need an escort home, they'll provide one for you. If they can't, they'll call a cab to pick you up (and they'll pay for it, too). **Campus police walk the campus** checking up on the security of all the buildings. All the dorms are locked down, and only the people who live there can get in. Guests have to be escorted."

Q "Campus is pretty secure. I don't know if that's because **the University tries to make it safe** with things like security guards and blue-light phones, or if I feel safe since no matter what time of night you are out, there are always people walking around."

Q "You need to use your **ID card to get into the dorms**, and they only work at the dorm where you live. If you don't live there, your friend's supposed to let you in and be with you all the time, but that usually doesn't happen."

The College Prowler Take On...
Safety & Security

Security is a constant concern on the Penn State campus. Dorms are now on 24-hour lockdown and students must have their ID cards handy in order to enter. While dorm lockdown does make it harder for any random person to wander in, students do use their cards to bring in outside friends, and often let strangers in by politely holding the door, assuming they live there. The best way to be safe is to use common sense: allow only people whom you know live in the building, and lock your dorm room door when you are not there and while you are sleeping.

There are well-placed blue-light emergency phones around campus, and the student police services are friendly and helpful at all hours. At night, however, there are few police patrolling the campus. The presence of the State College police is strongly felt downtown, especially during the weekends. Police cars patrol the streets looking for blatantly drunk kids and out-of-control parties. Although the local police seem overbearing at times, with officers in cars, on foot, or riding horses down the streets, it's important to remember that they are concerned about everyone's safety. On home football weekends, the population nearly doubles from the influx of fans and tourists, so students are not the only concern of patrolling officers.

B+

The College Prowler® Grade on

Safety & Security: B+

A high grade in Safety & Security means that students generally feel safe, campus police are visible, blue-light phones and escort services are readily available, and safety precautions are not overly necessary.

Computers

The Lowdown On...
Computers

High-Speed Network?
Yes–Ethernet

Wireless Network?
No

Operating Systems:
Mac OS, Unix/Linux,
Windows

Number of Labs:
49

Number of Computers:
4,649

Free Software

Eudora, Netscape, HostExplorer, WS_FTP, PDF Viewer, Ping, and TimeSync utilities

Discounted Software

None

Charge to Print?

Students are allotted 110 free pages from the labs.

Did You Know?

Penn State not only has computer technicians in their labs, but also in the commons of every dorm area to serve your personal computer, as well. **ResCom (Residential Computing)** will come to your dorm room and troubleshoot any problem you may be having with your hardware or software. For more info, visit: *www.rescom.psu.edu.*

Students Speak Out On...
Computers

"You have access to cable anywhere on campus and at all the apartment buildings. The labs usually aren't too packed, but they can be a hassle if you need to get things done fast."

Q "**The computer labs are very accommodating**, and you rarely have to wait; although bringing your own computer is certainly more convenient, as you can do most tasks from the comfort of your room."

Q "**Definitely have your own computer**. The labs are not always crowded, but there is nothing like having your own computer and printer when you need it. And the Ethernet card allows access to an excellent high-speed network that has suited my needs for three years."

Q "There is an extensive computer network. **Some labs are crowded**, but this is more of a social issue than anything—they are the popular labs to go to. However, there are always going to be open computers; you just have to choose the right lab. Bringing your own computer is completely optional. You can easily get along without one, but it is a lot more convenient, and Ethernet is provided in the dorms for fast connections."

Q "**There are six main computer labs on campus**. They're always open for any student to use, and in each lab there are technicians to help you with any problem that you might have."

Q "Labs are always crowded, but **the machines here are top notch**."

Q "The computer network is great, but there is traffic in the labs. Sometimes you wait, sometimes you don't. But there are tons of computer labs located throughout campus, so **you don't really need to bring a computer** unless you like working in the comforts of your own room."

Q "Plan on bringing your own computer. Even though the **computer labs are pretty good**, having your own computer will be more convenient for everyday work. Plus, it's great to have a computer just for communicating with other students. Computer labs are usually only crowded during the beginning and end of the semester, and whenever big projects are due (like around midterms and such). The general purpose labs are usually not as packed as the college-specific labs, which can be ridiculously crowded at times."

Q "**The network is good**; you have a nice fast connection in the dorms . . . when it's working. The PSU network is notorious for cutting out just when you need to log on to get an article or right in the middle of downloading a bootleg of *The Matrix*. There are so many computer labs that, unless it's the week before finals when everyone has projects due, you won't have a problem finding a spot to do your work."

Q "Having your own computer definitely makes research and work a little easier, but there are usually some **computers available in the computer lab**."

The College Prowler Take On...
Computers

The computer network is a fast and convenient way to stay connected to both the Internet and campus resources. Every student gets his or her own Ethernet connection already built into the dorm room. Once you register your Ethernet card (available in the student bookstore if you don't already have one) with ResCom, you're up and running! The total registering process usually takes two or three days. There has been a recent crackdown on file-sharing programs, as they are usually illegal, depending on whether or not you actually pay for your program. To prevent students from stealing music, Penn State actually provides a subscription to Napster to each student living in the dorms, which they can use should they bring a computer to campus.

The computer labs are a decent alternative to having your own computer. Though they do get crowded, there is nearly always a computer available or a very short wait to use one. There is a lab located in every dorm area. However, the convenience and privacy of having your own computer in your dorm room is undeniable. The ability to communicate with your friends, classmates, and professors at all hours without leaving your room is one that should seriously be considered by anyone thinking of leaving their PC or Mac at home.

The College Prowler® Grade on

Computers: B

A high grade in Computers designates that computer labs are available, the computer network is easily accessible, and the campus' computing technology is up-to-date.

Facilities

The Lowdown On...
Facilities

Student Center:
The HUB Robeson Center

Athletic Center:
The White Building
The IM Building
The Natatorium

Libraries:
17

Campus Size:
10,099 acres

Popular Places to Chill:
The HUB; it's where everyone congregates on campus during the day, between classes, and for nighttime activities.

What Is There To Do on Campus?

The HUB is one of the most popular spots on campus, where students can get a bite to eat or chill out with friends. To kill some time, there is the Corner Pocket pool room, the Center for Arts & Crafts, and Late-Night Penn State, which shows movies and has presentations on a weekly basis. Another popular spot in the warmer months is the Creamery. Students often boast that its the best ice cream you can find.

Movie Theater on Campus?

Free movies are shown during the weekends at the HUB, the Kern Building, the Carnegie Building, and the Chambers Building in addition to any faculty or club-sponsored film nights. There is a regular movie theater downtown, and three more in the surrounding area.

Bowling on Campus?

No

Bar on Campus?

No

Coffeehouse on Campus?

Yes! Campus offers several coffeehouse options, including Otto's Café in the Kern Building, MacKinnon's Café in Pattee Library, Java Markets at several campus locations, and Starbucks in the HUB.

Favorite Things to Do

There are so many students and so much going on at any given moment, it's hard to narrow it down to a few favorites. Students really enjoy just relaxing with friends over coffee or beers, playing one of the many sports available on campus, or catching the latest movie, event, or speaker at the HUB.

Students Speak Out On...
Facilities

{ **"The facilities on campus are above-average. Most of the facilities are handicap-friendly, and there are computer centers most every corner of the campus."**

Q "The White Building gym is the most widely-used gym facility, and it is way-overcrowded. It is sometimes hard to fit in a workout when you are always waiting for machines. But **all gyms are in convenient locations** throughout campus."

Q "**All of the facilities here are really nice**, and they are relatively new. There are plenty of places for sports, and there's just always somewhere to go."

Q "**The facilities are really good here**. There are different gyms on campus for basketball, volleyball, and weightlifting—all that the YMCA has to offer—and then some. The student union (the HUB) was newly renovated a few years ago and is very modern. There are fast food joints, places to study, convention rooms, an art gallery, and a record-breaking fish tank. It's a very popular hangout."

Q "Many facilities are pretty much brand new. **The HUB is great**. It has a Starbucks, Panda Express, Sbarro's, Chic-fil-A, a deli, hamburger joint, and a taco place. There are three indoor pools and four on-campus gyms, two of which are pretty new. There have been talks of putting a climbing wall in, too, but for now, they put a temporary one up every Friday in the HUB. If you want to be active, you'll have no problem doing it here."

Q "The student center was just remodeled a couple of years ago. It's pretty awesome, in my opinion. The facilities, overall, are in really good shape. On the downside, it seems like they are always doing some kind of construction on campus, but a lot of construction shows that **the University is expanding**, and that's a good thing in my mind. Computers in the labs are very good, I think, and are often updated as PSU finances permit."

Q "**The facilities on campus are very well-kept**. The buildings are always neat and clean, and the landscaping is always well kept."

Q "Facilities are very nice on campus. There are tons of athletic centers with a good bit of equipment; one low price provides access for the semester. The girls that work out there are unbelievable! Computer labs are pretty well taken care of, and computers are upgraded about every two years or so. The HUB is very nice, and lots of people use it for studying, eating, and meeting with groups or friends. **The HUB also has a lot of late-night activities** on the weekend if drinking isn't your forte."

Q "The HUB is **a teenage wasteland** come to life."

Q "**The facilities at Penn State vary in quality**. Some of the computer labs are really nice, and the same goes for the athletic facilities and the HUB. The White building is shiny and new, and the old gym at Rec Hall is not quite as new and pretty, but it is still functional. The same goes for the computer labs. The HUB was remodeled not too long ago, and it is a great place to curl up and sleep between classes."

The College Prowler Take On...
Facilities

The student center, known as the HUB, is one of the nicest buildings on campus. It is not only visually attractive, but it's an epicenter for all kinds of student activities. The HUB houses various fast-food spots, a Starbucks coffee kiosk, an art gallery, study lounges, game rooms, an auditorium where free movies are shown on the weekends, and an Alumni Hall used for everything from blood drives to free concerts. Despite the fact that athletics play such an integral part of Penn State life, sports and recreation facilities simply aren't up to par with those of other large universities. The main gym is often crowded during the day, and it is not unusual to stand in line for a machine. If you want to work out regularly, it's a good idea to consider a smaller gym or a workout schedule that will help you avoid the crowds. Penn State does have every type of facility available to students: Olympic-sized swimming pools, full gyms, ice rinks, tennis courts, and more. University facilities are also kept clean and well maintained.

The presence of construction machinery is a reflection of Penn State's continuing efforts to expand and keep itself up-to-date with other major state colleges. In the midst of a rural area, the University is an island of new technology and modern resources.

B+

The College Prowler® Grade on
Facilities: B+

A high Facilities grade indicates that the campus is aesthetically pleasing and well-maintained; facilities are state-of-the-art, and libraries are exceptional. Other determining factors include the quality of both athletic and student centers and an abundance of things to do on campus.

Campus Dining

The Lowdown On...
Campus Dining

Freshmen Meal Plan Requirement?

Yes

Meal Plan Average Cost:

$1,480

Places to Grab a Bite With Your Meal Plan:

The Big Onion

Location: Findlay Commons, 1st floor

Food: Pizza, cheesesteaks, salad, sushi

Favorite Dish: Cheesesteak

Hours: Monday–Thursday 7 a.m.–12 a.m., Friday 7 a.m.–10 p.m., Saturday 9 a.m.–10 p.m., Sunday 9 a.m.–12 a.m.

→

Bluespoon Deli

Location: Warnock Commons, 2nd floor

Food: Breakfast, grill, salads, subs, online sub orders

Favorite Dish: Grilled cheese

Hours: Monday–Thursday 7 a.m.–10 p.m., Friday 7 a.m.–9 p.m., Saturday– Sunday 11 a.m.–9 p.m.

Café Laura

Location: Mateer Building

Food: Full, elegant restaurant

Favorite Dish: Chicken cacciatore

Hours: Monday–Friday 7:30 a.m.–1:30 p.m.

Findlay Dining Commons (East Halls)

Location: Findlay Commons, 2nd floor

Food: All-you-can-eat American, international, vegetarian, vegan

Hours: Daily, 11 a.m.–2 p.m., 4:30 p.m.–7:30 p.m.

Fresh Express

Location: Findlay Commons, 2nd floor

Food: Healthy á la carte items, salads, wraps, smoothies, Mongolian-style grill

Favorite Dish: Ceasar wrap

Hours: Monday–Thursday 11 a.m.–1 p.m., 5 p.m.–8 p.m. (Closes Friday 7:30 p.m.)

Good 2 Go

Location: Findlay Commons, 1st floor

Food: Conveneince store

Favorite Dish: Ben & Jerry's ice cream

Hours: Daily, 10 a.m.–1 a.m.

Harriet's Hideaway

Location: McElwain Hall, 1st floor

Food: Bagel sandwiches, cookies, ice cream, salads

Favorite Dish: Turkey bagel sandwich

Hours: Monday–Friday 7 a.m.–9:30 a.m., Thursday– Sunday 8 p.m.–12 a.m.

Louie's

Location: Redifer Commons, 2nd floor

Food: Convenience store, late-night snack bar

Favorite Dish: Snickers bar

Hours: Monday–Friday 7 a.m.–1 a.m., Saturday– Sunday 9 a.m.–1 a.m.

McElwain Dining Hall (South Halls)

Location: McElwain Hall, lower level

Food: All-you-can-eat, eggs-to-order, make-you-own waffle station, Healthy Horizons

Favorite Dish: Omelette

Hours: Monday–Friday 7 a.m.–10:30 a.m., 11 a.m.– 1:30 p.m., 4:30 p.m.–7:30 p.m.

Moxie (Coffee Bar and Store)

Location: Waring Commons, 1st floor

Food: Coffee, pastries, smoothies (Lounge also has Playstations, Internet bar, and TV)

Favorite Dish: Strawberry smoothie

Hours: (Coffee Bar) Monday–Thursday 7 a.m.–1 a.m., Friday 7 a.m.–10 p.m., Sunday 6 p.m.–1 a.m.

(Store) Monday–Friday 7:30 a.m.–1 a.m., Saturday 11 a.m.–10:30 p.m., Sunday 11 a.m.–1 a.m.

Otto's Café

Location: Kern Building

Food: Coffee, baked goods, sandwiches, grill

Favorite Dish: Grilled chicken sandwich

Hours: Monday–Thursday 7:30 a.m.–5 p.m., Friday 7:30 a.m.–3 p.m.

Pollock Dining Commons

Location: Pollock Commons, 2nd floor

Food: All-you-can-eat, eggs-to-order, Tina's Muffins, Big Daddy's Deli, rigaTony's

Favorite Dish: Club sandwich

Hours: Monday–Friday 7 a.m.–9:30 a.m., 11 a.m.–2 p.m., 4:30 p.m.–7 p.m., Saturday 11 a.m.–2 p.m., 4:30 p.m.–7 p.m.

Redifer Dining Commons (South Halls)

Location: Redifer Commons, 2nd floor

Food: All-you-can-eat (Southside Buffet), pizza, subs, stir-fry, salads,

Favorite Dish: Pepperoni pizza

Hours: (South Food District) Monday 7 a.m.–9 p.m., 11 a.m.–9 p.m., Saturday 11 a.m.–9 p.m.

(Southside Buffet) Monday–Friday 11 a.m.–1:30 p.m., 5 p.m.–7:30 p.m., Sunday 11 a.m.–1:30 p.m., 5 p.m.–7:30 p.m.

Roxy's

Location: Findlay Commons, 2nd Floor

Food: '50s-style American

Favorite Dish: Cheeseburger, chocolate shake

Hours: Monday–Friday 7 a.m.–9:45 a.m., 11:30 a.m.–2:30 p.m., 4:30 p.m.–7 p.m.

Simmon's Dining Hall (South Halls)

Location: Simmons Hall, lower level

Food: All-you-can-eat, salad bar, pizza, desserts, McKean St. Deli

Favorite Dish: Cobb salad

Hours: Monday–Friday 11 a.m.–2 p.m., 4:30 p.m.–7 p.m., Saturday–Sunday 10:30 a.m.–2 p.m., 4:30 p.m.–7 p.m.

Union St. Marketplace

Location: HUB, 1st floor

Food: Food court;
Burger Co., Casa Ortega,
Chat's, Chick-fil-A, Higher
Grounds, Joegies, Mixed
Greens, Panda Express,
Piccalilli's, and Sbarro

Favorite Dish: Cheesesteaks
from Joegies (named in honor
of the Big Ten school's famous
football coach)

Hours: Vary, based on
individual vendors

Waring Square (West Halls)

Location: Waring Hall,
2nd floor

Food: All-you-can-eat, deli,
pasta, salad bar, pizza, stir-fry,
bakery, Veg Works

Favorite Dish: Cobb salad

Hours: Monday–Friday
7 a.m.–9:30 a.m., 10:30 a.m.–
2 p.m., 4:30 p.m.–7:30 p.m.,
Saturday–Sunday 10:30 a.m.–
2 p.m., 4:30 p.m.–7 p.m.

Warnock Dining Commons (North Halls

Location: Warnock Commons,
2nd floor

Food: All-you-can-eat, entrees,
salad bar, Asian, Italian

Favorite Dish: General Tso's

Hours: Sunday–Thursday
5 p.m.–7 p.m.

The West Wing

Location: Waring Hall,
2nd floor

Food: Salads, wraps,
sandwiches, desserts

Favorite Dish: Buffalo
chicken wrap

Hours: Monday–Friday
11 a.m.–8 p.m.

Off-Campus Places to Use Your Meal Plan:

The meal plan is not accepted
off-campus, but LionCash,
Penn State's declining debit
meal plan account, is accepted
off campus.

Student Favorites:

The Big Onion

Bluespoon Deli

Waring Square

The HUB

Otto's Café

Did You Know?

The Penn State Bakery offers all kinds of cookies and personalized cakes to celebrate any occasion. They can be ordered online, so parents can send their kids sweet care packeges.

The Creamery has made Penn State famous for homemade ice cream, frozen yogurt, and other great snacks. There are 110 flavors of ice cream to choose from!

There are **Java Markets by Java Company** scattered throughout campus. These stations include freshly-made sandwiches, salads, coffee, and other drinks. Stop by one of these locations:

Ag Science and Industries Building

Burrowes Building

Coller Café

East-Engineering Sciences

Gateway Café above Shortlidge

KC Café

MacKinnon's Café in Patee West

Resse's Café and Market in IST building

Campus Dining

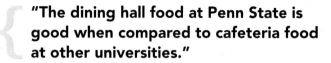

"The dining hall food at Penn State is good when compared to cafeteria food at other universities."

Q "**The food is excellent in the HUB** if one is willing to pay the price. The 10 percent discount that the HUB offers is not enough for most students. Food in the commons is generally nothing more than filling."

Q "Personally, **I am not a big fan of cafeterias**. I don't like the food, and there is always some form of chicken for dinner. In East Halls, there is a sandwich shop that is good. The Big O is good if you have it sparingly, but it is expensive. Elsewhere, Louie's in South is good for late-night meals, and the Bluespoon serves great wings and is pretty cheap for on-campus dining."

Q "**On campus, the best quality and variety is in the West Halls dining commons**. To grab a snack and do a little studying, Otto's Cafe in the Kern building is efficient and recently remodeled. The HUB has tons of perks—its central location makes it a good meeting spot. Even so, the HUB is best during non-peak hours."

Q "**There is quite a variety of food on campus**, and most of the restaurants are located in the HUB building. HUB food ranges from Mexican food to greasy, fast foods. The cafeteria food, however, isn't too appealing."

Q "**The cafeterias are the cheapest but also the crappiest dining places**. There are several sandwich shops, pasta places, and diners where you can also use your 'meal points.' Also, at the HUB there are fast food places like Panda Express, Sbarro Pizza, Joagie's Hoagies, Burger Co., a taco place, a coffee shop, and Chic-fil-A."

Q "Each dorm complex has its own cafeteria plus a few fast food places. I think all the food is pretty good here. In the West Halls, where all the older students live, food really is better than at home. They have a pizza bar, deli bar, salad bar, desert bar, and Chinese food at every meal. In East Halls, where the freshmen live, **the cafeteria food isn't as good, but the fast food is great**. They have the Big Onion for pizzas and strombolis, and Fresh Express for deli sandwiches. You can pay for it all with your meal card. Be careful though, your points will disappear pretty fast if you don't watch your spending. Take the bus down to West Halls if you want to eat well."

Q "Food on campus varies. If you room in East Halls, stay away from the food; it's cheap, but you get what you pay for. **The HUB, where all the students hang out, has really good food, but it's expensive**."

Q "The food is good here: **it is not mom's home cooking, but it's good**. West Halls is my favorite, but I love Checkers and Fresh Express in East Halls. The Creamery has such good-homemade ice cream. We also get micro-fridges in the dorms, and they're great."

Q "**I love the HUB** because it's like a giant food court in the middle of campus, and it's a great place to meet friends, discuss classes, and eat. We have a Starbucks and bagels, ice cream, burgers, Chik-fil-A, Ortega, Chinese, Sbarro pizza, Joagies, vending machines, and more."

Q "**Eh, food here is okay but nothing to brag about**. The Moxie in West Halls has great smoothies. The Bluespoon in North Halls has a Ben and Jerry's. North Halls is extremely close to the Creamery, which has good ice cream and is open late at night."

Q "The commons aren't too bad if you like chicken. It seems chicken is on the menu every night. I think they recycle it. But if you have to eat in a commons, go to Waring (West Halls). They have the best selection. There are also eateries in the HUB—**good food, fast, healthy, and unhealthy, just the way college kids like it**."

Q "Penn State has a **duality to its food selection**. On the one side, you have got some great food at West Campus and Myles. It has a large selection that ranges from everything to everything else. But if you're stuck in Warren Towers, then you have the lower end of the food. You've got the McDonald's burger compared to the filet mignon of West Campus."

Q "Food sucks here, but that's probably expected of most campuses. **East and West Halls have the best food and the most variety**. West is a bit of a nuthouse, though, and East is out of the way (unless you live there) and consists of mostly freshmen. East has a Big Onion, which is really good for the A-La Board food plan. North has Bluespoon, which is great for lunch. With a student plan, you can pay like $1–$2 for a full lunch, which is the cheapest anywhere."

Q "**You'll have no problem gaining your Freshman 15 here**. There's no way around it. The dining halls are fairly nice, but what else would one expect for $24,000 a year?"

Q "The food is actually surprisingly good. **The dining halls are humongous**, almost overwhelmingly so, and the food court is really decent for a university."

The College Prowler Take On...
Campus Dining

No college dining hall has ever been famous for its food quality—except, perhaps, on parent visitation day. Penn State is no exception. Some meals are universally enjoyed, while others will leave you gagging. The University's A-La Board meal plan is required for all undergraduates living in dorms. This plan is based on a "points" system: depending on the option you purchase, you get a number of points that can be used through your student ID to buy food on campus. The meal plan is not accepted elsewhere in State College, so it's best to set aside cash for the days you simply can't stomach more of the dining hall fare. The meal points can carry over from fall to spring semesters, provided you purchase another A-La Board plan within two weeks of spring term; however, this doesn't hold true for spring to summer terms. Any points leftover by the end of spring semester are forfeited. The size of the plan can be changed throughout most of the semester.

As far as food goes, no two halls serve the same menu. Depending on the size of the hall, options such as salad and pasta bars, stir-fry stations, and mini-bakeries may also be available. Each commons building also has a smaller alternative to the dining hall with different hours. There is also the HUB to fall back on, which is similar to a food court at a mall. There's Chinese, Italian, and Mexican fast food, a sandwich shop, a burger joint, and a café. The options here are endless. However, the HUB is probably the most expensive place to eat on campus.

The College Prowler® Grade on

Campus Dining: B

Our grade on Campus Dining addresses the quality of both school-owned dining halls and independent on-campus restaurants as well as the price, availability, and variety of food.

Off-Campus Dining

The Lowdown On...
Off-Campus Dining

Restaurant Prowler:
Popular Places to Eat!

Allen Street Grill
Food: American, fine dining
100 W. College Ave.
(814) 231-4745
www.allenstreetgrill.com
Cool Features: Upstairs from the Corner Room.
Price: $15–$25 per person
Hours: Daily, 11 a.m.–2 a.m.

American Ale House & Grill
Food: American, fine dining
821 Cricklewood Dr.
(814) 237-9701
www.americanalehouse.com
Cool Features: Piano entertainment on weekends.
Price: $15–$30 per person
Hours: Sunday–Thursday
11 a.m.–10 p.m., Friday–Saturday 11 a.m.–11 p.m.
(Open 'til 12 a.m. on football home-game weekends)

Baby's Burgers and Shakes
Food: American diner
131 S. Garner St.
(814) 234-4776
www.babysburgers.com
Cool Features: '50s
style diner.
Price: $4–$8 per person
Hours: Sunday–Thursday
11 a.m.–10 p.m., Friday–
Saturday 11 a.m.–12 a.m.

Brother's Italian Restaurant & Pizza
Food: Italian
204 E. College Ave.
(814) 234-9951
Price: $5–$10 per person
Hours: Daily, 10 a.m.–9 p.m.

Café 210 West
Food: American
210 W. College Ave.
(814) 237-3449
www.statecollege.com/mcc/ cafe210
Cool Features: Outdoor patio seating, live entertainment on weekends.
Price: $6–$10
Hours: Daily, 11 a.m.–2 a.m.

Champs Sports Bar & Grill
Food: American
1611 N. Atherton St.
(814) 234-7700
www.champssportsgrill.com
Cool Features: Seven areas for dining and lounging including a patio, loft, pool room, and garden room.
Price: $8–$15 per person
Hours: Daily, 11 a.m.–2 a.m.

Chili's Grill & Bar
Food: Southwestern
137 S. Allen St.
(814) 234-5922
www.chilis.com
Price: $12–$20 per person
Hours: Monday, Tuesday, Thursday 11 a.m.–11 p.m., Wednesday, Friday, Saturday 11 a.m.–12 a.m., Sunday 11 a.m.–10 p.m.

College Pizza
Food: Pizza
128 Locust Ln.
(814) 231-2000
Cool Features: Frequent specials; open late-night.
Price: $3–$6 per person
Hours: Monday–Wednesday 11 a.m.–2:30 a.m., Friday–Saturday 11 a.m.–3 a.m., Sunday 11 am.–10 p.m.

The Corner Room

Food: American

100 W. College Ave.

(814) 237-3051

Cool Features: The most famous restaurant in State College, right across from campus.

Price: $4–$10 per person

Hours: Daily, 7 a.m.–10 p.m.

D.P. Dough

Food: Italian, take-out, pizza

Address: 1460 Martin St.

(814) 237-4747

Price: $4–$8 per person

Hours: Sunday–Wednesday 11 a.m.–1 a.m., Thursday–Saturday 11 a.m.–2 a.m.

The Deli Restaurant

Food: American

113 Hiester St.

(814) 237-5710

Price: $7–$14 per person

Hours: Sunday–Wednesday 11 a.m.–12 a.m., Thursday–Saturday 11 a.m.–2 a.m.

Denny's Restaurant

Food: American

1860 N. Atherton St.

(814) 238-1644

Price: $6–$12 per person

Hours: Daily, 24 hours

Double D's

Food: Pizza

222 W. Beaver Ave.

(814) 237-9600

Price: $3–$7 per person

Hours: Monday–Saturday 11 a.m.–2 a.m., Sunday 11 a.m.–12 a.m.

Duffy's Tavern

Food: American

113 E. Main St., Boalsburg

(814) 466-6241

www.duffystavern.com

Cool Features: Catering available, micro/craft beers.

Price: $10–$20 per person

Hours: Monday–Saturday 11 a.m.–1 a.m., Sunday 11 a.m.–9 p.m.

Faccia Luna Pizzeria

Food: Italian

1229 S. Atherton St.

(814) 234-9000

www.faccialuna.com

Price: $9–$15 per person

Hours: Monday–Saturday 11:20 a.m.–11 p.m., Sunday 12 p.m.–10 p.m.

The Gingerbread Man

Food: American

130 Heister St.

(814) 237-0361

http://gmanstatecollege.com

(The Gingerbread Man, continued)

Cool Features: Nightly specials, outdoor dining, G-Man merchandise available.

Price: $7–$13 per person

Hours: Daily, 11:30 a.m.–2 a.m.

Golden Wok

Food: Chinese

332 W. College Ave.

(814) 234-1102

Cool Features: Probably the best Chinese food in town, in a finer restaurant atmosphere.

Price: $6–$9 per person

Hours: Sunday–Thursday 11:30 a.m.–10 p.m., Friday–Saturday 11:30 a.m.–11 p.m.

The Green Bowl

Food: Vietnamese

131 W. Beaver Ave.

(814) 238-0600

Cool Features: Make your own stir-fry.

Price: $5–$9 per person

Hours: Monday–Saturday 11 a.m.–9 p.m., Sunday 11 a.m.–8 p.m.

Gumby's Pizza

Food: Pizza

300 S. Pugh St.

(814) 234-4862

www.gumbyspizza.com

Price: $4–$8 per person

Hours: Monday–Wednesday 2:30 p.m.–2:30 a.m., Thursday 2:30 p.m.–3:30 a.m., Friday–Saturday 10:30 a.m.–3:30 a.m., Sunday 10:30 a.m.–1:30 a.m.

Herwig's

Food: Austrian

129 S. Fraser St.

(814) 238-0200

www.herwigsaustrianbistro. com

Cool Features: Austrian home cooking!

Price: $7–$12 per person

Hours: Daily, 11:45 a.m.–8 p.m.

Hi-Way Pizza

Food: Italian, take-out, pizza

340 E. College Ave.

(814) 237-5718

Price: $5–$8 per person

Hours: Monday–Wednesday 11 a.m.–10 p.m., Thursday 11 a.m.–12 a.m., Friday–Saturday 11 a.m.–3 a.m., Sunday 11:30 a.m.–10 p.m.

Hooters
Food: Wings, grill
538 E. College Ave.
(814) 272-4668
www.hooters.com
Price: $8–$12 per person
Hours: Daily, 11 a.m.–12 a.m.

India Pavilion
Food: Indian
222 E. Calder Way
(814) 237-3400
Cool Features: Indian lunch
buffet, party hall available.
Price: $9–$15 per person
Hours: Daily, 11:30 a.m.–2:30
p.m., 5 p.m.–10:30 p.m.

Irving's Bagels
Food: American, deli, brunch
110 E. College Ave.
(814) 231-0604
Cool Features: Best bagels in
town! Tori Amos ate here.
Price: $4–$6 per person
Hours: Daily, 7 a.m.–8 p.m.

Jimmy John's
Food: American, subs
220 W. College Ave.
(814) 234-6677
www.jimmyjohns.com
Cool Features: Open until
3 a.m.
Price: $5–$9 per person

(Jimmy John's continued)
Hours: Sunday–Wednesday
11 a.m.–12 a.m., Thursday–
Saturday 11 a.m.–3 a.m. (Hours
vary depending on customer
demand.)

Manhattan Bagel
Food: Bakery, café
3180 W. College Ave.
(814) 234-5540
www.manhattanbagel.com
Price: $4–$6 per person
Hours: Monday–Friday
5 a.m.–4 p.m., Saturday–
Sunday 6 a.m.–4 p.m.

Mario & Luigi's Restaurant
Food: Italian
1272 N. Atherton St.
(814) 234-4273
www.saucetoyou.com
Cool Features: Great
deserts! (Try the Chocolate
Intemperance.)
Price: $10–$20 per person
Hours: Monday–Friday
11:30 a.m.–2 p.m.,
4 p.m.–10 p.m., Saturday
11:30 a.m.–10 p.m.,
Sunday 12 p.m.–10 p.m.

Outback Steakhouse
Food: American
1905 Waddle Rd.
(814) 861-7801
www.outbacksteakhouse.com
Price: $15–$20 per person

(Outback Steakhouse, continued)

Hours: Monday–Thursday
4 p.m.–10 p.m.,
Friday 4 p.m.–11 p.m.,
Saturday 3 p.m.–11 p.m.,
Sunday 2 p.m.–9:30 p.m.

Panera Bread

Food: Bakery, café
148 S. Allen St.
(814) 867-8883
www.panera.com
Price: $5–$10 per person
Hours: Sunday–Thursday
7 a.m.–9 p.m., Friday–
Saturday 1 a.m.–10 p.m.

Papa John's Pizza

Food: Pizza
2110 N. Atherton St.;
1341 S. Atherton St.
(814) 238-7272,
(814) 234-7272
www.papajohns.com
Price: $4–$9 per person
Hours: (N. Atherton)
Daily, 11 a.m.–11 p.m.
(S. Atherton) Daily,
11 a.m.–9:30 p.m.

Perkins Family Restaurant

Food: American
1661 S. Atherton St.
(814) 235-1960
www.perkinsrestaurants.com
Price: $8–$15 per person
Hours: Daily, 24 hours

Red Lobster

Food: Seafood
1670 N. Atherton St.
(814) 867-3867
www.redlobster.com
Price: $10–$20 per person
Hours: Sunday–Thursday
11 a.m.–10 p.m., Friday–
Saturday 11 a.m.–11 p.m.

Spats Café & Speakeasy

Food: Fine Cajun, Creole
142 E. College Ave.
(814) 238-7010
www.spatscafe.com
Cool Features: Only Cajun
and Creole dining in town.
Price: $10–$15 per person
Hours: Monday–Thursday
11:30 a.m.–9:30 p.m.,
Friday–Saturday
11:30 a.m.–10:30 p.m.

Sports Café & Grill

Food: American
244 W. College Ave.
(814) 234-2294
Cool Features: Sports bar with
outdoor patio seating.
Price: $10–$15 per person
Hours: Daily, 11 a.m.–2 a.m.

The Tavern Restaurant

Food: American, fine dining
220 E. College Ave.
(814) 238-6116
Cool Features: Nice place to
take your parents.

➡

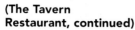

(The Tavern Restaurant, continued)

Price: $15–$25 per person

Hours: Monday–Thursday 5 p.m.–10 p.m., Friday–Saturday 5 p.m.–10:30 p.m., Sunday 5 p.m.–8:30 p.m.

V&S Sandwiches

Food: American, fast

128 E. College Ave.

(814) 861-8022

www.meatymadness.com

Cool Features: Holds a "free cheesesteak day" every fall.

Price: $4–$7 per person

Hours: Monday–Wednesday 10:30 a.m.–10:30 p.m., Thursday–Saturday 10:30 a.m.–3 a.m., Sunday 11 a.m.–9 p.m.

Waffle Shop

Food: American, breakfast

364 E College Ave.

(814) 237-9741

Price: $6–$12 per person

Hours: Monday–Saturday 6 a.m.–3 a.m., Sunday 7 a.m.–4 p.m.

Wing Zone

Food: Wings

433 E. Beaver Ave.

(814) 234-WING

www.wingzone.com

Price: $5–$10 per person

Hours: Monday–Thursday 4 p.m.–1 p.m., Friday 4 p.m.–3 a.m., Saturday 11 a.m.–3 p.m., Sunday 12 p.m.–1a.m.

Ye Old College Diner (the Diner)

Food: American

126 W. College Ave.

(814) 238-5590

www.thediner.statecollege.com

Cool Features: Consider themselves a Penn State tradition.

Price: $2–$7 per person

Hours: Daily, 24 hours

Best Pizza:

Best pizza? This is a very crucial and individual decision that you'll have to make for yourself once in State College. There is certainly no lack of options. There are a lot of different deals throughout the year, so be sure to pay attention to the annoying blue Valu-Paks that will be shoved into your mailbox. Here's a general guideline to your pizza delivery options:

Gumby's Pizza – Best Cheese Sticks (called Pokey Stix)

Papa John's – Best Overall Deal

D.P. Dough – Best Pizza Alternative (individual calzones, over 50 varieties, free soft drinks)

Best Chinese:
Golden Wok

Best Breakfast:
Waffle Shop

Best Wings:
Hooters

Best Healthy:
Green Bowl
Panera Bread

Best Place to Take Your Parents:
Allen Street Grill
Golden Wok
Mario & Luigi's Restaurant
The Tavern Restaurant

Other Places to Check Out:

Applebee's, Arby's, Brother's NY Style Pizza, Burger King, Cafe 201 West, Canyon Pizza, Damon's, Duffy's Boalsburg Tavern, Faccia Luna Pizzeria, McDonald's, McLanahan's Deli, Mio Zio, Mount Nittany Inn, Pennsylvania Pizza, Penn State Sub Shop, Quizno's, Ruby Tuesday's, Subway, Taco Bell, Wendy's, Zola New World Bistro

Closest Grocery Stores:

Giant
2222 E. College Ave.
(814) 861-2578

McLanahan's Downtown Market
116 S. Allen St.
(814) 861-3530

Wal-Mart Supercenter
1665 N. Atherton St.
(814) 237-8401

Wegman's Food Market
345 Lowe's Blvd.
(814) 278-9000

Students Speak Out On...
Off-Campus Dining

"There's quite a variety of food off-campus, but most restaurants are downtown. There's a Thai restaurant at the west end of campus and a few Asian restaurants scattered around."

Q "There are **tons of restaurants with reasonably-priced food** and a cool hangout/bar scene. The Deli, the Gingerbread Man, and the Sports Café are good examples."

Q "**College Pizza is the place to get pizza**. It costs around $4 for a college special! You get two huge slices of pizza, a breadstick, and a beverage. Come on, at three in the morning, when you're stumbling home, there's nothing better to put in your stomach."

Q "The Tavern, Mount Nittany Inn (for an expensive seafood buffet), and the Allen Street Grill are good for dinner. The Deli and the Corner Room are good for lunch. **The Waffle Shop is good for breakfast**."

Q "**The restaurants here aren't too shabby**. All the regular chains—McDonald's, BK, Subway, Damon's, and Red Lobster—are around. McLanahan's has cheap subs made to order. We all live on DP Dough and Papa John's delivery as well as late night pit stops at College Pizza or Canyon Pizza where it's 'a buck a slice.' The Penn State Sub Shop and Wing Zone are also really good wing joints."

Q "**We have over 20 pizza places**. Papa John's delivers pizza until 4 a.m. on weekends, Jimmy Johns deliver subs until 3 a.m. on weekends, and you can get Chinese food and frozen yogurt until 1 a.m. I love the Corner Room; it's a really nice restaurant, especially for dates. We also have Chili's and the Allen Street Grill (ASG), which is pretty fancy. There's Spats, which is somewhat more formal, but not as much as ASG. The Deli is also nice. We have a Wing Zone, which delivers until 2 a.m. on weekends and an Indian food restaurant, along with lots of other places."

Q "**There are many nationally-known restaurants** like Chili's, Ruby Tuesdays, Red Lobster, and Outback, but one of my favorites is a place called Baby's—it's like an old fashioned '50s diner. It is fun, and best of all, it's cheap!"

Q "Restaurants are located mostly off-campus. Mario and Luigi's, Café 210, the Tavern, the Corner Room, and the Allen Street Grill are all good places to eat. There are also ethnic restaurants that carry Indian, Thai, and authentic Mexican cuisine. **There's lots of variety to choose from here**."

Q "**A good Web site to check out is _www.psu.dailyjolt. com_**. While it's the opinion of a very limited amount of students, it is still a pretty good guide. On the site, you'll find information on what's going on campus, places to eat, concerts, the ride board, and other PSU-related stuff."

Q "**Most restaurants in State College are fabulous, but most are overpriced**. Expensive places like Spats, Zola's, and the Tavern are favorites that are usually for when parents want to take you out. Mediocre restaurants are everywhere like Applebee's, the Corner Room, and Mio Zio. And (naturally) we have our sketchy places—if you want your tea refilled with coffee, and obnoxious service at three in the morning, go to the Diner. Everyone does at some point."

Q "**Restaurants off campus are a hit-or-miss deal**. Some cater to the drunk (not good), others cater to the professors (expensive)."

Q "The restaurants here are **pretty decent**, although there isn't really an authentic Italian place in the area. There needs to be. The good spots are Spats, Faccia Luna, Duffy's, and Arby's."

Q "For some good pizza delivery, **Gumby's and Papa John's are always a crowd pleaser**. PA Pizza is a great place for a good pizza under $6. The Corner Room is a nice restaurant to go to with friends to eat and relax. And grilled stickies at the Diner are a must!"

Q "There are lots of good places to eat off-campus. Fast food (Wendy's, McDonald's, 8,000 Subways, Quiznos, Arbys, Taco Bell) and sit-down restaurants (Corner Room, the Deli, Baby's, Chili's, Brothers Pizza, Hi-Way Pizza, the Diner, and a bunch more I can't remember right now). **Don't expect to get any good service at the Diner, though**. I think they're actually trying their best to be known for their poor service. But that just gives us poor college students another reason not to tip."

Q "The restaurants in this town are good. **Everyone makes a big deal about the Corner Room** (a local landmark) but, frankly, I have never been impressed with the food. Spats is amazing if you have the money to afford it. A great place for an limited budget is the Green Bowl, a unique stir-fry restaurant. Chinese food is easy to come by here, but it's not necessarily good. Pizza is big in a college town like State College, and almost all pizza shops are acceptable for 2 a.m. cravings."

The College Prowler Take On...
Off-Campus Dining

Considering the small town atmosphere of State College, there are many international eateries and plenty that offer American food. If you wake up early enough, the Waffle Shop and the area's numerous family restaurants specialize in breakfast food (and, of course, some serve breakfast 24 hours a day, for those 3 a.m. pancake cravings). For lunch, a town staple is the Corner Room, which offers comfortable family dining. There are many diners around town—including Baby's, known for its 1950s theme, and Ye Old College Diner, world famous for grilled stickies and horrible service. For fine dining, the area also has a number of upscale restaurants. The Tavern is great for impressing a date or enjoying a meal you can't afford (when your parents come to visit, of course). The Green Bowl focuses on buffet-style healthy eating and is popular with vegetarians.

State College has a surprisingly large assortment of Chinese, Italian, and Indian restaurants. The Golden Wok and other downtown establishments offer a refreshing alternative to campus Chinese, while India Pavilion, Herwig's, and Spats have food to suit international tastes. About a thousand pizza delivery places exist and thrive. These pizzerias offer many specials—you will try all of them within the first semester and probably become fiercely loyal when you find the one that best suits you. The area surrounding State College offers a similar range of dining options. All but the pickiest eaters will find something to like off campus, and, if you do some exploring, you may even discover a new favorite food.

B

The College Prowler® Grade on

Off-Campus
Dining: B

A high Off-Campus Dining grade implies that off-campus restaurants are affordable, accessible, and worth visiting. Other factors include the variety of cuisine and the availability of alternative options (vegetarian, vegan, Kosher, etc.).

Campus Housing

The Lowdown On...
Campus Housing

Room Types:
Residence rooms include singles, doubles, triples, (sharing central bathrooms with floor) and suite-style units, as well as apartments (on- and off- campus; efficiencies, one-, or two-bedroom)

Number of Dormitories:
43

Undergrads Living on Campus:
36%

Best Dorms:
North Halls
West Halls

Worst Dorms:
East Halls
South Halls

Large Dormitory Residences:

East Halls
www.hfs.psu.edu/east

Halls: Bigler, Brumbaugh, Curtin, Geary, Hastings, McKean, Packer, Pennypacker, Pinchot, Snyder, Sproul, Stone, Stuart, Tener

Community: Primarily Freshmen

Room Types: Double

Features: Radio Station, Health Center, Bookstore, computer lab, University Learning Center, Good 2 Go, Roxy's, Fresh Express, the Big Onion

Special Living Options: FISE (First-Year in Science and Engineering), LIFE (Living in a Free Environment)

North Halls
www.hfs.psu.edu/nort

Halls: Holmes, Leete, Runkle

Community: Mixed

Room Types: Double

Features: Only area to offer all coed living, Bluespoon Deli, computer lab, game room, basketball courts, tennis courts, volleyball net, Palmer Art Museum, the Playhouse Theatre, Creamery

Special Living Options: AA (Arts and Architecture), BASH (Business and Society), Discover House, Earth House

Pollock Halls
www.hfs.psu.edu/pollock

Halls: Beaver, Hartranft, Hiester, Mifflin, Porter, Ritner, Schulze, Shunk, Wolf

Community: Mixed, several sorority houses

Room Types: Double

Features: Pollock Laptop Library, computer lab, Women's Health Clinic, the Mix, Greenberg Indoor Sports Complex, Eisenhower Auditorium

Special Living Options: EASI (Engineering and Applied Sciences), HEAL (Health Education and Awareness in Living), HAC (Helping Across the Community), ILH (International Languages), IST (Information Sciences and Technology), MLK (Martin Luther King, Jr. House for Social Justice), WISE (Women in Science and Engineering)

South Halls
www.hfs.psu.edu/south

Halls: Atherton, Cooper, Cross, Ewing, Haller, Hibbs, Hoyt, Lyons, McElwain, Simmons, Stephens

Community: Mixed, several sorority houses

Room Types: Double

Features: Closest to Downtown, three cining halls, Louie's, Healthy Horizons, Harriet's Hideaway, computer lab, indoor walkways, Schreyer's Honors College

(South Halls, continued)

Special Living Options: LIFE (Living in a Free Environment), Living and Learning Environments (Atherton and Simmons)

West Halls

www.hfs.psu.edu/west

Halls: Hamilton, Irvin, Jordan, McKee, Thompson, Watts

Community: Mixed, mostly Upperclassmen

Room Types: Regular double, small double, triple

Features: Center of campus, computer lab, food court, West Wing, study lounge, Moxie, Electronic (internet and gaming) Lounge, outdoor patio and café, Rec Hall, Otto's Café, Lion Shrine

Special Living Options: EMS (Earth and Mineral Sciences), STS (Science, Technology, and Society)

On-Campus Apartments:

Eastview Terrace

www.hfs.psu.edu/eastview

Halls: Brill, Curry, Harris, MIller, Nelson, Panofsky, Young

Community: Upperclassmen

Coed: Yes, both single-gender and coed houses

Room Types: Singles

Features: Close to Bryce Jordan Center, Beaver Stadium, McCoy Natatorium, dining facilities, mail service, residential computing

Nittany Apartments & Suites

www.hfs.psu.edu/nittanyapts

Community: Upperclassmen

Coed: No

Room Types: Singles

Features: Optional meal plan, close to McCoy Natatorium, Pollok Commons, tennis courts, track and field facility, Greenberg Indoor Sports Complex, Eisenhower Auditorium

Bed Type

Single, extra-long

Cleaning Service?

Yes, 5 days a week

You Get

Beds, bookshelves, bulletin boards, chests of drawers, closets, desks and chairs, Ethernet connections, microwave/microfridge combination unit, trash can, TV hookup (cables not included)

Did You Know?

Complimentary copies of the *New York Times*, *USA Today*, *Centre Daily Times*, and the *Daily Collegian* are available for all residents every weekday in your dorm building's lobby.

"The dorms are horrible. They're dirty and small. However, the nicest dorms are in West Halls and the dorms in the Honors College."

Q "The dorms are nice. West is the nicest, but East is where they stick freshmen. I lived there for two years and loved every minute of it. It was more fun living with people going through the same thing I was. Pollock is close to town, and **South is run by sororities**."

Q "East is a great place for freshmen to live and meet other freshmen. **West is the nicest dorm**, but it is too quiet and uneventful for me. South is in a great location (right on College Avenue) and has decent-size rooms. Pollock has a great location and fairly large rooms."

Q "**The freshmen dorms (East Halls) resemble little prison cells**. I would recommend enduring them, though, because it is all freshmen housing. You meet a lot of people and make friends. West has the best rooms, but the kids there aren't as friendly. You look forward to off-campus housing after the mandatory freshman year in the dorms."

Q "The dorms are adequate here. **As a freshman, you want to live in East with the entire freshmen class**, but after that I would recommend Pollock or South."

Q "The dorms are fun here. **All freshmen should try to get into a coed dorm**, and have fun with everyone in the building."

Q "**The dorms are pretty nice**. West is probably the nicest, but as a freshman you would stay in East. It is the closest to football games, but farthest to class. However, everyone gets used to it, and everyone bonds there."

Q "I think the dorms here are decent compared to other large universities. **The best dorm, in my opinion, is Simmons (in South Halls)**. The second best dorms are in West Halls."

Q "East is very small, but that's where all the freshmen live. If you don't know a lot of people, you will meet kids your age there. West Halls dorms are big and house mostly upperclassmen. **Pollock is convenient and houses mainly sophomores and some freshmen**. South Halls has lots of honors kids. North Halls has music and arts majors."

Q "**East and South** are particularly wretched."

Q "North is not as far away from everything as East, but its quiet. They have coed floors. **West and South are the most popular because they are closer to the town**."

Q "I don't think any of the dorms are bad, but **the most liked by students would probably be West Halls**. Regardless, they all allow students to interact, get to know one another, and build some life-long friendships."

Q "**Dorm life is essential—literally**. You can't live off-campus the first year of school. East is far, but it's nice if you want to be around freshmen. North is quiet but small. West is big, has nice food, but is a bit anti-social. South is almost all sororities, but it is close to the frats and downtown."

Q "Eh, dorms are dorms. Dorms at PSU are nothing really to rave about, but **if you get stuck in East, good luck**."

Q "Considering all the parts of campus that are constantly being built or remodeled, facilities here vary greatly. Some of the dorms (West and parts of South) are like hotels. **Nittany apartments are quite nice, but they're hard to get into** if you aren't an athlete. Rooms in East, North, Pollock, and parts of South are made of standard concrete block that's not really big enough for two people to live in. Still, that's what college is all about. South is full of sororities, East is all freshmen, and West is stereotypically anti-social."

The College Prowler Take On...
Campus Housing

The dorms at Penn State vary widely in size and quality. In the campus housing booklet that advertises each dorm area, East Halls comes across as the best dorm. This is where nearly all incoming freshmen end up, but student opinion will tell you that it's, by far, the worst dorm. East Halls are probably the least attractive clump of buildings on campus. They are the farthest from central campus and downtown, and the rooms are the smallest. You could think of living your first year in these dorms (affectionately referred to by students as "the projects") as a college initiation. West Halls is probably the best housing area and is located in the center of campus. The buildings are picturesque and joined together by lovely lawns and walkways. West also houses the largest and nicest dining halls within the commons, as well as a large computer lab, café, and a lounge with video game systems. Freshmen don't usually get in, but it is something to consider for campus housing later on.

Penn State's campus housing meets the needs of the student body. Many students agree that off-campus housing is the most desirable option. If you plan to make the most out of dorm life, however, upperclassmen have access to the nicest living facilities available.

The College Prowler® Grade on

Campus Housing: B

A high Campus Housing grade indicates that dorms are clean, well-maintained, and spacious. Other determining factors include variety of dorms, proximity to classes, and social atmosphere.

Off-Campus Housing

The Lowdown On...
Off-Campus Housing

Students in Off-Campus Housing:

64%

Average Rent For:
1BR Apt.: $685/month
2BR Apt.: $960/month
3BR Apt.: $1,300/month

Popular Areas:

Downtown

Best Time to Look for a Place:

October, early November

Students Speak Out On...
Off-Campus Housing

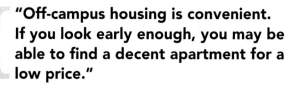

"Off-campus housing is convenient. If you look early enough, you may be able to find a decent apartment for a low price."

Q "Living off-campus here is very convenient. There are many places that are very close to campus. I lived in an apartment where the **rent was about $300 per month** per person, and everything was included, except phone and parking."

Q "Off-campus housing is definitely less expensive than on-campus housing. **Just be patient and shop around**. There are great places where you can have your own bedroom and lots of space. But there are high rises where they squeeze three of you into one bedroom. Hunt the apartments located in houses and stay away from any buildings in Beaver Canyon."

Q "**I would say 80 percent of off-campus housing is in a great location, even for walking distance**. The major apartment buildings are a block or two from campus, and bus transportation runs right down Beaver Avenue. The apartments near Wal-Mart are farther, but not many undergraduate students live there."

Q "**Off-campus housing is convenient enough**. There are lots of nice apartment buildings either a block or two away from campus. Some aren't too expensive. Finding a house to live in is a little more difficult, and they are usually farther away from campus."

Q "**There are lots of apartments, houses, fraternity houses, and townhouses to choose from**. They are pretty expensive because the tyrannical landlords know they can feed off the college kids who want to get out of the dorms, but it's still cheaper than the University's room and board for dorms."

Q "**There are plenty of places to live**. It's worth it if you don't mind cooking or cleaning for yourself . . . or walking an extra ten minutes to campus."

Q "I'm living in an apartment next year, and I'm so excited. It is downtown, so it's close to campus. There are apartments available that are bigger but farther away, so you'd have to take a bus or drive. I have friends who live there. They like the extra space, but **it's a benefit to live closer to school**."

Q "**Living off-campus is definitely worth it**. It provides you with a whole different experience than living in the dorms. There are so many apartment complexes around that finding somewhere to live is pretty easy."

Q "After freshman year, get an apartment! Choose wisely, though. **Start your search in October and sign the lease in late November**. Otherwise, there won't be anything good left. Keep in mind bus schedules and class location. They are pricier downtown, but it is worth it."

Q "**Get the hell off-campus after your freshman year**. It's cheaper and you can shower without shoes on."

Q "Off-campus housing is only worth it after at least two years of being on campus. **There is a rush to get off-campus housing as soon as the year begins**, so by the time you're thinking of looking around by the end of freshman year, you probably won't get anything."

The College Prowler Take On...
Off-Campus Housing

Penn State requires freshmen to live in the residence halls, so off-campus housing doesn't become an option until sophomore year. Even then, spending another year in residence halls isn't such a terrible idea. The conditions do get better, and you can enjoy the benefits of dorm life—not cooking or cleaning—for a little longer before you make it into the real world. For the first year, you're thrown together with a roommate not of your choice. By the second year, however, most students have formed their own circle of friends and can choose to live in neighboring dorm rooms to create the perfect dorm environment. If you do choose off-campus housing, you'll probably end up only slightly farther from classes than your dorm.

Many of the student-friendly apartments are in downtown State College, which is either a short walk or bus ride from campus. As you go farther out, the apartment sizes increase and rents decrease. It isn't uncommon for students to get townhouses around State College and commute to campus. This means you either have to bring your own car or become familiar with the bus schedule. The biggest advantage of living outside the dorms is the freedom it gives you. This can be a great learning experience. It is the first time many students have to deal with buying food, keeping up with bills, and maintaining their own place. While some would prefer to use their meal points in the dining commons rather than fight over whose turn it is to do the dishes, there is satisfaction in eating food you've cooked for yourself. Provided you're willing to take on the extra responsibility and alter your lifestyle a little, living off-campus can also be significantly cheaper than dorm life and meal plans.

B+

The College Prowler® Grade on

Off-Campus
Housing: B+

A high grade in Off-Campus Housing indicates that apartments are of high quality, close to campus, affordable, and easy to secure.

Diversity

The Lowdown On...
Diversity

Native American:
0%

White:
84%

Asian American:
6%

International:
2%

African American:
4%

Unknown:
1%

Hispanic:
3%

Out-of-State:
23%

Political Activity

Campus has a more liberal leaning, but that doesn't mean other groups don't voice their opinions as well. When a social issue becomes particularly heated, there are often rallies and protestors representing all sides. The steps of Old Main and the end of the mall on College Avenue are the most popular places to find student activists.

Gay Pride

Homosexuality can be a sensitive issue at any campus. Through such organizations as Allies and the USG Department of LGBTA Affairs, the gay community actively participates and often spearheads debates and events promoting acceptance, understanding, and safe sex.

Minority Clubs

Penn State has about 50 minority clubs and student organizations run by and directed to students of many different cultures and nationalities. These clubs sponsor different events across campus and sometimes become highly visible in local media; a good example is the Black Caucus, which frequently makes news as it strives for racial equality on campus.

Most Popular Religions

There are about 46 active religious organizations on campus, the majority of which is affiliaPted with Christianity. For a full listing, please visit the Student Organizations section on page 146 of this book.

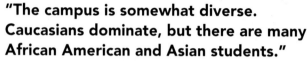

Students Speak Out On...
Diversity

> **"The campus is somewhat diverse. Caucasians dominate, but there are many African American and Asian students."**

Q "The Penn State campus is not that diverse, actually. Most of the students are white, and **many students come from states around Pennsylvania**. However, minorities do have several organizations and participate in all athletics and academic programs."

Q "The campus isn't very diverse because it is in the middle of nowhere. **There are only a small percentage of minorities on campus**."

Q "This is your **typical, white, suburban** college campus."

Q "**Everyone here is white and from Pittsburgh or Philadelphia**. The only diversity we have is among our professors; they come from all around."

Q "**Diversity is basically the only thing that students feel Penn State doesn't have**. There have been many racial issues here, but administration and faculty are working hard on making PSU more diverse."

Q "**I feel very comfortable here on campus**. Compared to my home in New Jersey, there are less Hispanics and more African Americans on campus. That's the only big difference. There are over 20 religious groups to my knowledge, too."

Q "Penn State is not very diverse racially. There is an equal distribution of men and women, though. **There are some minorities**, but the vast majority of Penn State students are white, and you can see the lack of diversity when you take a walk through campus."

Q "Culturally, Penn State is very diverse. Overseas, it is an extremely popular university to attend, so **it attracts students from many countries around the world**. Chances are, you will have several international students in every class, which provides for a much more dynamic and culturally-diverse discussion."

Q "With Pollocks, Italians, Pennsylvanians, West Virginians, and others, **it's really a convergence of cultures**. Oh yes, and everyone's white."

Q "Sometimes it seems too diverse here, like **the school lets in dumb people from all over the country** just to get more money. I thought I was going to a school that chose people for their academics, not their heritage."

Q "Penn State is the **melting pot of PA**."

Q "Sure, the campus population is very diverse—**there are people of various shades of white, at least**."

Q "**Almost everyone is white and middle class or a farmer**. Every so often you get that foreign student or someone from Philly or Pittsburgh but, in reality, PSU is not very diverse."

The College Prowler Take On...
Diversity

Penn State's campus is mostly made up of white middle-to-upper class Pennsylvanians. Although white Pennsylvanians are very nice people, you may desire more variety among your peers. Both the Black and Latino Caucuses work especially hard at keeping high profiles and bringing cultural events to Penn State. Through the annual Mr. and Ms. Black Penn State, keynote speakers address pertinent issues, while programs such as "The Miseducation of Generation X" poke fun and shoot holes through racial and gender stereotypes. Obviously, the call for a more diverse Penn State is often heard.

Overall, Penn State reports a very low incidence of hate crime on or around campus. It's important to keep in mind, however, that State College is surrounded by rural areas with an even less diverse population. The climate is by no means adverse to minorities, but it may not be as accommodating as larger cities and more diverse college towns. The political leaning of central Pennsylvania is generally conservative. While different cultural and personal backgrounds are accepted around campus, this may not be the case when you're away from the University's grounds. More liberal residents agree that the best way of dealing with the close-mindedness of the area is through education and tolerance. Recent statistics have indicated that minority populations are increasing at Penn State, but they have a long way to go before the campus could be considered a modern day "melting pot."

The College Prowler® Grade on

Diversity: C

A high grade in Diversity indicates that ethnic minorities and international students have a notable presence on campus, and that students of different economic backgrounds, religious beliefs, and sexual preferences are well-represented.

Guys & Girls

The Lowdown On...
Guys & Girls

Men Undergrads:
54%

Women Undergrads:
46%

Birth Control Available?

Yes, University Health Services, Ritenour Building
(814) 949-5540

Most Prevalent STDs on Campus

HPV

Social Scene

Most students quickly find their own social niche on campus, whether it's partying downtown four nights a week, or spending the weekend at the game fairs in the HUB. The majority of the students seem to prefer the former. Though the HUB is packed on weekends and the free movies can be difficult to get into at times, the downtown scene, frats, and apartment parties are more popular. Penn State is a party school, and students largely turn to drinking for their entertainment.

Hookups or Relationships?

Relationships have been known to happen on campus, of course, but on the average Friday or Saturday night, many students seem to look for Mr. or Mrs. Right Now, rather than Mr. or Mrs. Right.

Best Place to Meet Guys/Girls

The best place to go out and meet new people is Players Nite Club (the name says it all). Even in subzero temperatures, the girls are out in tanks and minis, and the guys follow suit with light linen pants and tiny muscle shirts. Unfortunately, Players is the only dance club in town; if it's not your type of scene, you're left with the bars and random house parties. There are lots of bars around campus. Some of the more popular bars include Café 210 West, the Sports Café, the Darkhorse Tavern, and the Rathskellar.

Dress Code

Everyone at Penn State follows his or her own personal style. Casual, Bohemian, Preppy, Goth, and the like—there isn't really an overriding style (though you can see PSU clothing everywhere you look, especially on football weekends). The popular trends generally follow those of the rest of the country. Downtown is home to Abercrombie & Fitch, Gap, American Eagle, Eddie Bauer, and a number of private shops —especially Metro—that carry the "trendy necessities."

Students Speak Out On...
Guys & Girls

"The guys seem to be far more immature than the girls. Most guys don't like serious dating, so if you're looking for a relationship, good luck! And obviously, the girls are cute!"

"I don't know about guys, but **there are a few decent girls here and there**."

"For kids from Pennsylvania, New York, New Jersey, and Maryland, **the girls are pretty darn good looking**. Visiting other schools, I realize how spoiled I am."

"There are a lot of good-looking girls here, and it's always nice to see how **the girls go out to filthy house parties in their skimpiest attire**. It's kind of funny also."

"Well, I'm attached, but there is definitely a variety, and **parties here can look like *People* magazine**."

"Well, being a guy, I feel that I am great. Now, I don't know if that gives the whole feel of the campus, but **there are good guys to be found**. As for the girls, there are the 'sorostitutes,' and yes, there are a lot of good-looking women."

"**The women here are gorgeous**. There are lots of beautiful people, but it's not even that. I've found people want to be happy being themselves. People here want to be fit. I don't consider myself gorgeous by any means, but I love the people I have made friends with."

Q "**There are some mighty fine guys here**, but there are also some not-so-fine ones."

Q "**There are a lot of good-looking women on campus**: blondes and brunettes, as well as girls from all races and countries."

Q "With a huge student body of 40,000 people, you are going to find your hot ones, but you are also going to find your not-so-hot ones. **It is difficult to describe girls or guys as anything**, since there are so many different people and personalities."

Q "People are the same at PSU as they are at all campuses as far as I'm concerned. **They are all full of themselves!**"

Q "**Everyone is hot! Just not as hot as me, of course**! Just kidding. Truthfully though, I'm sure if you come, you won't be disappointed."

Q "Well, I am a guy, and I must say that there are so many hot girls on this campus, **it's not even funny**! I mean, everywhere you go, from class, to a frat party, even walking down the streets, you see hot girls. The only downside here is that all the girls are white, so **there isn't much variety across races and ethnicities**."

Q "**The guys, especially the athletes, are extremely hot!**"

Q "**The girls here are all pretty stupid. The guys are hot, but also stupid**. The girls here are fat, but they decide to dress slutty anyway. Like Jon Stewart said: 'Forty-thousand 20-year-olds in the land of cows? You guys must get drunk and fornicate every night!' And it's true—there are free condoms at the AIDS Project."

Q "Good looking guys at Penn State? **Sad state of affairs**."

Q "There are so many young people on campus, you are bound to find someone that you like. There is no shortage of hot people, either. **Come spring, hot people come out of hiding**."

The College Prowler Take On...
Guys & Girls

Considering that there are 40,000 young people on campus, you're bound to find someone you think is hot, and vice versa. If there's no one in your immediate vicinity, keep your eyes open during class, at the HUB, and downtown. Girls tend to take more pride in their appearance (or are just more interested in attracting attention) than guys do, so they tend to be better looking and generally have a more "put-together" appearance. On a Thursday, Friday, or Saturday night, the majority of girls get pretty dressed up, guys make themselves presentable, and people look to meet each other.

True to the party school stigma, students seem to lean towards "hookups" or casual relationships, rather than more serious connections. It's also been a tradition that the student body gets hotter in the spring, when clothes come off and the lawns are crowded with sunbathers, athletes and others. You must remember that with the amount of alcohol flowing through Penn State, it can become difficult to figure out who's hot and who isn't, regardless of what conventional standards or common sense might tell you.

The College Prowler® Grade on Guys: B

A high grade for Guys indicates that the male population on campus is attractive, smart, friendly, and engaging, and that the school has a decent ratio of guys to girls.

The College Prowler® Grade on Girls: B+

A high grade for Girls not only implies that the women on campus are attractive, smart, friendly, and engaging, but also that there is a fair ratio of girls to guys.

Athletics

The Lowdown On...
Athletics

Athletic Division:
Division I

Conference:
Big 10 Conference

School Mascot:
Nittany Lion

**Males Playing
Varsity Sports:**
444 (2%)

**Females Playing
Varsity Sports:**
287 (2%)

➜

Men's Varsity Sports:

Baseball
Basketball
Cross-Country
Diving
Fencing
Football
Golf
Gymnastics
Lacrosse
Soccer
Swimming
Tennis
Track & Field
Volleyball
Wrestling

Women's Varsity Sports:

Basketball
Cross-Country
Diving
Fencing
Field Hockey
Golf
Gymnastics
Lacrosse
Soccer
Softball
Swimming
Tennis
Track & Field
Volleyball

Club Sports:

Badminton
Basketball
Bowling
Crew
Cross-Country
Field Hockey
Flag
Football
Golf
Handball
Racquetball
Rugby
Soccer
Softball
Squash
Swimming
Tennis
Rack
Volleyball
Wrestling

Intramurals:

Basketball
Bowling
Cross-Country
Field Hockey
Flag
Football
Golf
Handball
Kayaking
Racquetball
Soccer

(Intramurals, continued)
Softball
Swimming
Tennis
Track
Volleyball
Wiffleball

Athletic Fields

Jeffrey Field, Beaver Field, and Softball Field

Getting Tickets

Tickets are free for all sporting events except basketball, football, gymnastics, women's volleyball, and wrestling. For these events, call 863-1000, or visit *www.psu.edu/sports/ tickets*.

Most Popular Sports

Football, women's basketball

Overlooked Teams

Any team that isn't the football team

Gyms/Facilities

Stadium, golf courses, ice skating rinks, indoor sports complex, field house, intramural building, wrestling room, basketball and volleyball gymnasiums, jogging track, racquet-sport and tennis courts, natatorium with fitness loft and indoor swimming pool, outdoor track, recreation building with multiple courts, weight room, rifle range, dance studios

Penn State Academic Support Program

Held in the Elliot H. Cole Academic Support Center, this program assists student-athletes in their academics and is available to all varsity student-athletes. There are ten desktop computers, all networked to the University and the Internet, four laptops, and a laser printer.

Walter A. Brown Area Memorial Skating Pavilion

The pavilion has a capacity of 3,806 and serves as the home of the Penn State hockey team. It is considered one of the finest facilities of its kind in the nation.

Students Speak Out On...
Athletics

"Varsity sports are very big on our campus because Penn State is Division I, which means that in order to participate in PSU sports, you have to have a scholarship or be an absolutely amazing athlete."

Q "Varsity sports are great. The **school spirit** when a sports team is doing well is tremendous."

Q "**Football games will send a chill down your spine** when you attend your first game. And everyone I know who is involved in IM sports meets a great group of people through it and has a great time."

Q "**Sports are huge but none more than varsity football**. The school is insane for those games, and they are so much fun. IM sports are available and are fun, also."

Q "Sports are big; **this is Penn State, folks**."

Q "Penn State football and JoePa reign supreme. **At PSU, tailgating is a contact sport**. We have championship volleyball, soccer, fencing, and hockey, as well."

Q "Basketball has had it's moments for the men, and the women's team is up there with UConn and Tennessee. IM sports are really big, too; **you can find a league for pretty much any sport** you can dream of."

Q "State College is the third largest city in Pennsylvania during home football weekends. **I have never seen so many campers**."

Q "Sports are a huge part of the school. The football games are so much fun; **I recommend getting tickets**. If you don't play varsity, though, there are tons of club and IM sports you can join."

Q "Varsity sports are huge, all of them. **It's awesome to go to such a great variety of sports events**. The IM sports are also big, and there are tons of sporting events going on in the fall, winter, and spring."

Q "**Varsity sports are huge**, especially football. IM sports are not as big, but they do get pretty competitive."

Q "Basically there's football, then there's everything else. **Football seems to have a stranglehold on Penn State**, which may be good or bad depending on how you look at it. Other varsity sports are overshadowed by it, but are, by no means, non-existent. IM sports are pretty big in that there are tons played all over campus all year long."

Q "Sometimes it seems like varsity sports are PSU. **In the fall, life is all about football games and tailgating**, and in the winter, I hear we have a basketball team. Football games are fun, but as you can see, you can be a PSU student and not care about sports."

The College Prowler Take On...
Athletics

Football is a big part of Penn State life. Other varsity sports pale in comparison to the aura of intensity that surrounds every home football game. People fly in from all over the country to sit in the 104,000-seat Beaver Stadium. Tailgating is a full-time, three day occupation. The town really comes alive with the influx of Penn State families and visitors during a game weekend, but you can avoid this by staying on campus. You don't have to love football to come to Penn State, but you do have to accept that Penn State loves football.

If, for some insane reason, you'd prefer a sport other than football, Penn State does offer just about every IM sport from whiffleball to kayaking. Some are more popular than others, but players aren't out to win popularity contests—only to enjoy a game. IM sports are an outlet for students, a hobby to indulge in that doesn't always carry the pressure of varsity competition. Although cheering the varsity teams to victory is important for many, the best way to experience the excitement and competition of sports is to participate yourself. Penn State provides a great environment for this, no matter what your choice of activity might be.

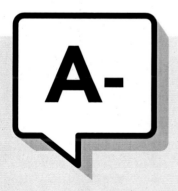

A-

The College Prowler® Grade on

Athletics: A-

A high grade in Athletics indicates that students have school spirit, that sports programs are respected, that games are well-attended, and that intramurals are a prominent part of student life.

Nightlife

The Lowdown On...
Nightlife

Club and Bar Prowler:
Popular Nightlife Spots!

The All-American Rathskeller

208 S. Pugh St.

(814) 237-3858

www.theskeller.com

The Rathskeller is located in a dark basement and known for cheap drinks and an electric atmosphere. Thanks to Spats Café upstairs, the Skeller is also home to some great food.

The Brewery

233 E. Beaver Ave.

(814) 237-2892

www.thebreweryinc.com

Overall, it's a very small joint, and it doesn't have the best ventilation—definitely a place to avoid if you don't like smoke-filled rooms. Home to frequent live performances and open-mic nights, you can also find frequent drink specials throughout the week. The fair variety of on-tap beer is served in mason jars, and there are also bottles available for take-out.

Café 210 West

210 W. College Ave.

(814) 237-3449

*www.statecollege.com/mcc/
cafe210*

For many Penn State students, the Café is a frat away from frat. Known as "the place to be" on Friday nights in many circles, the Café is also known for less-than-wonderful service and large waiting lines during peak hours. Nevertheless, the outdoor patio seating (except for the worst winter months, of course) is a great draw, and many feel comfortable within the packed atmosphere and large student population. The Café also offers an extensive food menu for late night munchies or midday meals.

Crowbar

420 E. College Ave.

(814) 237-0426

www.crowbarlivemusic.com

The Crowbar is State College's premier live music venue—it draws bigger acts than any of the local bars, and it isn't nearly as expensive as shows at the nearby Bryce Jordan Center. Be prepared to wait in long lines for the bigger-name bands.

Darkhorse Tavern

128 E. College Ave.

(814) 237-0490

www.darkhorsetavern.com

Located across from campus, the Darkhorse has a low-key atmosphere similar to the Brewery and the Phyrst. The Darkhorse has a reasonably large menu and hosts live music from local bands throughout the week.

The Phyrst

111 E. Beaver Ave.

238-1406

The Phyrst is State College's second-oldest bar, with 15 beers on tap and live entertainment nearly every night. Conveniently located on Beaver Avenue, it's only a few blocks from campus and centrally located in downtown State College. Phyrst's unique, Irish themed atmosphere has given it a strong following throughout the region.

Players Nite Club

112 W. College Ave.

(814) 234-1031

Players isn't just the best dance club in State College—it's the only dance club in State College. The events tend to be the same on a weekly basis, but it's a big draw nonetheless simply because it's the only game in town. Many Penn State students end up there throughout the week, so it's

(Players Nite Club, continued)

a good place to meet people. The club also hosts under-21 nights, which is one of the few chances underage students have to get involved in the "bar atmosphere" of the town.

The Saloon

101 Heister St.

(814) 234-0845

The Saloon has more of a "party" atmosphere than many of the area bars; it plays host to live music, karaoke, and DJs during the week, and offers a variety of special mixed drinks. These drinks, including "Monkey Boys," are big sellers and a great way to start the night. Monkey Boys are available in many flavors and served in pitchers topped with a handful of alcohol-soaked cherries.

The Sports Café

244 W. College Ave.

(814) 234-2294

www.statecollege.com/ sportscenter

The Sports Café is home to a game room, pool tables, and dart boards. Many special events can be found during the sports season, making this the venue of choice for athletes and sports fans.

Tony's Big Easy

129 S. Pugh St.

(814) 231-4590

www.tonysbigeasy.com

The Big Easy is the place to go for martinis, mojitos, and sophisticated drinks. This place caters to the more upscale crowd, though it doesn't take itself too seriously. Nightly drink specials and an evening menu keep students frequenting this campus bar.

Zeno's

100 W. College Ave.

(814) 237-2857

Zeno's carries what is probably the largest selection of beer in the entire region. This bar is known for its friendly atmosphere, and it offers live music most weekends; these make for an interesting contrast with the dark, smoky basement atmosphere. Zeno's is located right across from campus, and the food comes straight from the Corner Room!

Other Places to Check Out:

Adam's Apple

Chumley's

Lion's Den

Mad Mex

Otto's Pub & Brewery

Shandygaff Saloon

Student Favorites:

The G-Man (see Off-Campus Dining)

Players Nite Club

The All-American Rathskeller

Cheapest Place to Get a Drink:

G-Man with $2 pitchers

Players with $1 mixed drinks many Thursday and Friday nights.

Bars Close At:

2 a.m.

Useful Resources for Nightlife:

www.latenight.psu.edu

http://statecollege.com/bartour

The Weekender (published Fridays by the Centre Daily Times)

The Bar Tour at 9 p.m. on radio 101.1FM

www.happyvalley.com/ entertainment/bars.cfm

Nightlife Scene

There are only two clubs in State College: Players is the DJ dance club, and the Crowbar is the live music club. Both are pretty cool, within easy walking (or stumbling) distance from campus, and host special events occasionally. However, these two clubs are nowhere near enough to keep the large student population interested weekend after weekend. Expect long waiting lines no matter when you go, and no matter what temperature it is outside!

Unlike clubs, bars are plentiful in State College. Some are sports oriented (the Sports Café), others have an Irish theme (the Phyrst), and some are just cool, trendy places to hang out (Café 210 West). The bar scene is probably of more interest to students simply because there are enough bars to constitute a "scene." Most students learn the bars pretty quickly, as 21st birthdays are carried out in a grand bar tour tradition

What to Do If You're Not 21

If you're a freshman girl, the frat parties will welcome you in with open arms, but they may not be your best option simply for that reason. The HUB offers alternatives, such as games, dance classes, crafts, shows, and free movies on the weekends. Some of these can be a great way to spend an evening, while others leave much to be desired; basically, this depends on the weekend and your personal tastes. The University updates its weekly events on the Web, and their site can be found at *www.latenight.psu.edu*. Penn State tries to provide a range of options, and these are definitely worth checking out; there are always some good places to go with friends.

Players has an under-21 night, and Crowbar does have shows for all ages. In addition, keep aware of what is coming to both the Eisenhower Auditorium, or if a good band is playing at the Jordan Center—these shows are notoriously expensive, however. In the past, everything from Broadway musicals such as *Rent* and *Bring in da Noise, Bring in da Funk* to world-class dancer Gregory Hines and comedian Jon Stewart have come to Eisenhower Auditorium. Penn State's Rec Hall, though used less frequently now, has also been host to music acts such as Everclear, the Red Hot Chili Peppers, Guster, and George Clinton. For these events, student tickets are usually pretty cheap, and the shows are well done.

Student plays and other performances can be seen at the Pavilion Theatre, the Playhouse Theatre, and Schwab Auditorium, all conveniently located on campus. For more goings on in the arts scene, check out the *Centre Daily Times*'s *Weekender* magazine, the *Daily Collegian*, or the PSU Arts Web site at: *www.psu.edu/ur/arts.html*.

Students Speak Out On...
Nightlife

"**The bars are great off-campus, such as the G-Man, Cafe 210, and the Big Easy. The clubs leave something to be desired— there is only the cheesy Players. A large dance club might satisfy an un-met State College demand.**"

Q "The club scene, a.k.a. Players, has a happening atmosphere that's great for dancing and has good drink specials. And there are plenty of bars that are all diverse enough to **attract a particular crowd of students**. The bars with the type of atmosphere I like (dance music, spacious, don't smell like an ashtray, and more upscale) are the Gingerbread Man, the Big Easy, and Café 210 West."

Q "**The bars here are a must once you turn 21**. Try Adam's Apple for an Original Sin or the Big Easy (a.k.a. the Big Sleazy) for late-nights when you're too drunk to care how much you're spending on a drink. You have to be 21, though, unless you have an amazing fake ID. The bouncers at local bars get paid for confiscating fake IDs, and most bars have a scanner."

Q "There are quite a few bars off-campus with State College being a university town. The Lion's Den, Cafe 210, and the Sports Café are pretty popular spots. **They are really strict about IDs here**, so if you're not 21, I wouldn't mess with a fake ID. The rule of thumb is to hit Players twice a year, the first Tuesday of every semester, because that's when everyone shows up to see who's who."

Q "**Don't even try getting into clubs unless you are 21**! Some places to try include G-Man, the Saloon, Cafe 210, the Phyrst, and the Darkhorse."

Q "**Clubbing pretty much sucks here**. There is really only one place, and it's always too crowded, in my opinion. There are quite a few bars, at least 20 within walking distance. These provide good times when you're 21."

Q "I don't know about the bars, but I have a friend who works at the Shandygaff and says he loves it there. As for clubs, Crowbar is excellent; they get a lot of great bands and singers. On the weekends, **kids tend to go to fraternities or apartments**. I probably went to Players five or six Tuesdays this semester. They get a good crowd."

Q "There is one club called Players. **If you like wearing next-to-nothing** and dancing with trashy guys, then it's for you. Otherwise, stay away."

Q "Apartment parties are the best, and on any given weekend they can be found, quite literally, in the hundreds. **Bars off-campus are alright but, overall, pretty sketchy**. Places like the Sports Café and Café 210 West let you drink outside. Others, like the Phyrst, Rathskeller, and Chumley's, let you pack yourself into a small room and drink yourself stupid."

Q "If frat parties are your thing, then there are plenty of those. Be careful, though, because once rushing is over with, the **frat boys can be real idiots** and stop letting many people into their parties. Parties on campus are a bit non-existent, but if you have a circle of friends that like to throw parties, and an RA that doesn't care, then they can be pretty good. Some fun bars include the Saloon, Sports Café, Café 210, and the Phyrst."

Q "State College on a weekend (meaning Thursday through Saturday nights) is **like Mardi Gras**. The rest of the week is like a slow Mardi Gras with some classes thrown in. During the fall, the town is invaded by 100,000 drunken alumni for football games, and during the rest of the year, it's only the students who are drunk. Most people go off-campus to party, mainly at apartments and frats. Once you are legal, you can go to the bars, of which there are many. My personal favorites are Café 210, Crowbar, and the Saloon. Players is sketchy and full of drunken skeezes looking for someone to take home so they can wake up in bed together and introduce themselves."

Q "**Parties on campus usually consist of frat parties and wild house parties**. The bars downtown are great, especially in nice weather when you can sit out at the G-Man or the Café."

Q "Bars and clubs are awesome. **I absolutely love State College nightlife**. There is Players nightclub and the Crowbar. Lots of good bands play at the Crowbar."

Q "On-campus parties? When you find one, let me know. **Bars off campus are great**—there's one for every type of student."

The College Prowler Take On...
Nightlife

Parties on campus only happen at frat houses, and they aren't for everyone. Frat parties at PSU aim to attract freshmen girls or those in a sorority. Parties don't happen at sorority houses because there aren't any—sororities set up shop in the dorms or take over a floor of a building. Apartment parties are usually fun. Occasionally they do get busted, so underagers need to be careful, but, for the most part, apartment parties are harmless fun. There are many bars close to campus, but only two clubs: Players for dancing and the Crowbar for music. The Crowbar, which hosts most of the area's live music, tries to bring small and large acts to State College on a regular basis, as well as radio station-promoted events. This is a cool place to go when a band you like is playing, or to check out new bands.

Penn State tries to compensate for the local atmosphere by offering a lot of different activities through the HUB late at night. Many students do take advantage of what the HUB has to offer. However, the University simply can't offer enough for a large student population crammed into a small area. The lack of night life accounts for the large drinking problem at Penn State, and, while the town is mostly safe, it is impossible to avoid roving groups of drunken students after 10 p.m. The best advice for finding things to do around State College is to find a group of friends and be creative; everyone is in the same situation, and many choose not to drink. As a result, some of the best times can be had outside of bars and large parties.

B-

The College Prowler® Grade on

Nightlife: B-

A high grade in Nightlife indicates that there are many bars and clubs in the area that are easily accessible and affordable. Other determining factors include the number of options for the under-21 crowd and the prevalence of house parties.

Greek Life

The Lowdown On...
Greek Life

Number of Fraternities:
55

Number of Sororities:
259

Undergrad Men in Fraternities:
14%

Undergrad Women in Sororities:
11%

→

→

Fraternities:

Acacia
Alpha Chi Rho
Alpha Epsilon Pi
Alpha Gamma Rho
Alpha Kappa Lambda
Alpha Phi Alpha
Alpha Phi Delta
Alpha Rho Chi
Alpha Sigma Pi
Alpha Tau Omega
Alpha Zeta
Beta Sigma Beta
Beta Theta Pi
Chi Phi
Chi Psi
Delta Chi
Delta Kappa Epsilon
Delta Phi
Delta Sigma
Delta Tau Delta
Delta Theta Sigma
Delta Upsilon
Kappa Alpha Order
Kappa Alpha Psi
Kappa Delta Rho
Kappa Sigma
Lambda Chi Alpha
Lambda Phi Epsilon
Lambda Theta Phi
Phi Delta Psi-H

Phi Delta Theta
Phi Gamma Delta (FIJI)
Phi Kappa Psi
Phi Kappa Tau
Phi Kappa Theta
Phi Mu Delta
Phi Sigma Kappa
Pi Kappa Alpha
Pi Kappa Phi
Pi Lambda Phi
Sigma Alpha Epsilon
Sigma Alpha Mu
Sigma Chi
Sigma Lambda Beta
Sigma Nu
Sigma Phi Epsilon
Sigma Pi
Sigma Tau Gamma
Tau Epsilon Phi
Tau Kappa Epsilon
Tau Phi Delta
Theta Delta Chi
Theta Chi
Triangle
Zeta Beta Tau
Zeta Psi

→

Sororities:

Alpha Chi Omega
Alpha Delta Pi
Alpha Kappa Alpha
Alpha Kappa Delta Phi
Alpha Omicron Pi
Alpha Phi
Alpha Sigma Alpha
Alpha Xi Delta
Chi Omega
Delta Delta Delta
Delta Gamma
Delta Zeta
Gamma Phi Beta
Kappa Alpha Theta
Kappa Delta
Kappa Kappa Gamma

Lambda Delta Omega
Pi Beta Phi
Phi Mu
Sigma Delta Tau
Sigma Gamma Rho
Sigma Kapp
Sigma Lambda Gamma
Sigma Lambda Upsilon
Sigma Omicron Pi
Sigma Sigma Sigma
Zeta Phi Beta
Zeta Tau Alpha
Zeta Psi

Students Speak Out On...
Greek Life

"Greek life controls Greek students, as well as the bars when there are no Greek parties. There is no way any one group could drive the entire social scene here."

Q "Penn State has a **reputation for being a Greek school**, but I definitely don't think that Greek life is the social scene. I am in a fraternity, and I have just as many friends that are not Greek as I do that are. Either way, you can definitely find fun things to do every night. I also think that once you are old enough to go to the bars, Greek life also isn't as big."

Q "If you are involved in Greek life, then it runs the social scene until everyone is 21. **Greek life is a great way to narrow a Big Ten University to a smaller atmosphere**. I personally am thankful to Greek life for allowing me to interact with so many individuals. However, Greek life can also be a trap for people who get involved for the wrong reasons."

Q "Greeks dominate the social scene to a certain extent. **Frat guys are morons**, and girls go to parties because they can get free beer when they're not 21. Guys might as well not even waste their time at the frat houses; they won't serve you. Everybody who is 21 just goes to the bars, while the frat guys continue to hit on freshmen."

Q "**Greek life is pretty big at PSU**, especially at events like THON and the Homecoming Parade."

Q "**Frats are fun to go to your freshman year**, but it gets tiresome after a while, having to practically show frat guys your boobs just to get a beer. They're fun, but by sophomore year, unless you join a sorority, they just don't have the same appeal. One other thing, if you really are thinking about joining a sorority, we don't have any sorority houses here; they live in the dorms on campus."

Q "**Greek life isn't the only thing to do by any means**. There are a lot of apartment parties and stuff. I am not a big fan of Greek life because some brothers and sisters think they are better than everyone else. You find your niche here."

Q "**I personally hate the Greek system**, but it is very large and they do a lot of great things. I wouldn't say students have to join to have a social life, but Greek life tends to be a large factor here."

Q "**We have more frats and sororities than any other campus**, but not the highest percentage for enrollment. Frats supply free alcohol so kids go there on weekends, but it's not necessary to pledge."

Q "I am not in a sorority, and I have some friends who are in one and some who aren't. It's all about what you want. If you choose to rush and pledge anywhere, **there is a large selection of organizations** to choose from which is a bonus."

Q "The frats are huge (the buildings, not the numbers). **Frats usually keep to themselves and try to lure in freshmen girls**. Otherwise, you would hardly notice they even exist, unless you are into that type of thing."

Q "Greek life is big but not overbearing. **I got sick of it halfway through my freshman year,** and it never really bothered me since then—except for having to deal with the occasional dumb frat boy."

Q "Greek life is present definitely, especially during Homecoming and THON. **There is plenty to do here if you aren't in a frat or sorority**. I've been to my share of frat parties, and, honestly, I would always find myself wanting to be at an apartment party. There's more alcohol and music, and less scary people."

The College Prowler Take On...
Greek Life

Although Penn State has a huge number of fraternities associated with the University, only about 25 percent of students are involved in Greek life. The sororities do not have much social influence because they do not have their own houses, and thus have far fewer public functions. Frat houses are packed on the weekends, but there is always more going on downtown. If you join a fraternity or sorority, Greek life will obviously dominate your social scene, otherwise it has no great hold over the campus, and there's certainly no pressure to join. For those who choose to participate, the Greeks can offer many opportunities for fun and service. If Greek life isn't your forte, you certainly don't have to worry about feeling left out at Penn State.

Greek life at Penn State is generally positive, and fraternities and sororities offer a lot to the campus in the way of community service work. For example, the largest student-run charity in the nation, THON, is a 48-hour dance marathon organized by the Greek chapters. Each year, THON raises around three million dollars for children with cancer and is a universal source of pride among Penn State students.

The College Prowler® Grade on
Greek Life: A

A high grade in Greek Life indicates that sororities and fraternities are not only present, but also active on campus. Other determining factors include the variety of houses available and the respect the Greek community receives from the rest of the campus.

Drug Scene

The Lowdown On...
Drug Scene

Most Prevalent Drugs on Campus:

Ecstasy

Marijuana

Liquor-Related Referrals:

577

Liquor-Related Arrests:

410

Drug-Related Referrals:

82

Drug-Related Arrests:

102

Drug Counseling Programs

Centre County Drug & Alcohol
Willowbank Building, ground floor
420 Holmes St
Bellefonte, PA 16823
(814) 355-6744

Community Help Centre
139 S. Pugh St.
State College, PA 16801
(814) 237-5855

Counseling & Psychological Services
221 Ritenour Building
(814) 863-0395

Drug & Alcohol Intervention
University Health Services
234 Ritenour Building
(814) 863-0137

Students Speak Out On...
Drug Scene

> **"Drugs are present, but in no way are they dominating. Drug pushers try to stay in hiding, as Penn State is very anti-drug."**

Q **"If you are involved in the drug scene, it can get quite large**. But when you are out of the loop, it's hard to know what's really going down."

Q "There is a lot of pot around; nothing too hard, though. **There is some 'E' and coke around**, but it's not open."

Q **"Weed is big**, and a bunch of frats just got busted for an ecstasy ring."

Q "I really wouldn't know because **I would rather drink** than do any other drug."

Q "It's not a big problem. **If you look for it, it's there**. But I dare say that the drug scene is more prominent in my hometown than away at school."

Q "I really don't know; I don't do them. I know two kids that do, and they don't do it often. **There is high alcohol use**—I'm guilty of it—but I always have so much fun while being responsible. Whatever you do, be responsible, and you'll never have to worry."

Q "You can find drugs if you want them, but they do not run rampant. **It's not like dealers are selling crack in the library**."

Q "Oh, plenty of people do drugs, not as much as a bigger city school, though. **It isn't too bad**. The people who do choose to use drugs tend to stick to themselves."

Q "I suppose **the drug scene is big enough to get what you want**, if you want it, but not so big that you'll be forced into it."

Q "Penn State is mostly a drinking school—**alcohol is our drug of choice**. People get cited for underage drinking almost daily, and every weekend, the nearby hospital gets to deal with half a dozen alcohol poisonings. It is not uncommon to find puke on the steps of your dorm on Sunday morning, or to only have half your class present Friday morning because of excess partying Thursday night. However, there are still plenty of people who experiment with anything you can think of. A few favorites are pot and mushrooms, but cocaine and acid are not uncommon. The west side of town is known to be a pot area, while the east side consists of frats and reeks of alcohol."

The College Prowler Take On...
Drug Scene

Illicit drugs are available and relatively easy to get, but by no means have they taken over State College. The most prevalent drugs around campus are pot and ecstasy, though others exist in the area as well. The former may be a nuisance if you happen to live in a dorm room that overlooks an entrance used for smoking, and the latter is usually confined to bars and other off-campus areas. Penn State is pretty straight when it comes to illegal drugs, and every student has the chance to make his or her own decision. Drug problems are kept fairly well out of sight. The local government and police force are not tolerant of illegal substances and make an effort to crack down on both individual users and drug rings. Despite the bad publicity these few "drug busts" get in the local media, the area really doesn't have a large drug problem—especially when compared to many neighboring regions and cities.

Alcohol is a problem for both the campus and the surrounding area, especially during football weekends. Every year, there seem to be at least a few incidents of students suffering from alcohol poisoning or drinking-related accidents. Once again, these are avoidable as long as you know how to drink responsibly and avoid those who aren't; a little common sense goes a long way in Penn State's drinking culture. Even if you choose not to drink, you will be affected by it. Keeping a level head is the best way for everyone to stay safe and have fun.

The College Prowler® Grade on

Drug Scene: B+

A high grade in the Drug Scene indicates that drugs are not a noticeable part of campus life; drug use is not visible, and no pressure to use them seems to exist.

www.collegeprowler.com

Campus Strictness

The Lowdown On...
Campus Strictness

What Are You Most Likely to Get Caught Doing on Campus?

- Downloading copyrighted materials
- Drinking underage
- Indecent exposure
- Making too much noise in your dorm room
- Parking illegally
- Vandalizing the historic buildings
- Walking home drunk

Students Speak Out On...
Campus Strictness

"Officers are strict about drugs, and they try to cut down on the drinking as much as possible. They certainly don't let substance abuse slide by. You'll find that 98 percent of all parties occur off campus."

Q "Security isn't very strict at PSU. **If you can hide your evidence very well, you can get away with anything.**"

Q "Drinking in apartment buildings and fraternities at a reasonable noise level is generally **not subjected to being broken up by the police.**"

Q "**They are very strict concerning drugs and not so much about alcohol.** As long as you don't do anything idiotic, they won't bother you."

Q "Campus police are harsh when it comes to drugs and drinking. **The town police feast on the underage.** All of the frats are in town, so the police just wait for a drunk college kid to give them a reason to breathalyze them."

Q "If you were to be caught with drugs, I would imagine they would be pretty strict. With under-21 drinking, **you get three strikes while living on campus until you are kicked out**, but you can definitely drink on campus without getting in trouble."

Q "Drinking on the streets—especially on game weekends and events like Arts Fest—**is not tolerated.**"

Q "Don't try to buy alcohol with a fake ID or try to get into clubs if you're underage, because you will definitely get caught. **They're strict about public drunkenness**, too."

Q "**I was caught drinking in a dorm, and I had to go to a class to learn why drinking is bad**. It was no big deal, though; it was only an hour long."

Q "Oh yeah, be careful here at PSU. **You are definitely safe from any outside crime**, but you aren't safe from campus police trying to crack down on anything illegal."

Q "**Be really careful with campus police**. They revolve around trying to arrest students."

Q "**Campus police are pretty strict**. They can kick you out of PSU if they catch you with your pants down."

Q "**The police are definitely out to make the campus safe** and not to bust students."

Q "The police? You mean the people on horseback who watch you walk home drunk? **Just don't throw anything at them while you are pissed-off, and you'll be fine**."

Q "**The police here are somewhat lax**, but it depends on who you run into and how obvious you are"

Q "**People get busted for underage drinking all the time**. It's usually when they do something stupid though, like peeing on a public street or throwing snowballs at a cop car. If you are caught on campus, chargers will not usually be brought up, and you will just have to go through a campus drinking class."

The College Prowler Take On...
Campus Strictness

Campus authority at Penn State can be strict. Pranks, illegal acts in the dorms, and more are taken very seriously, and the University will make an example of students who are caught. While the University police are rarely the source of student complaints, they're not known for being sympathetic. It's best to keep your on-campus nonsense quiet, or else move it downtown.

When it comes to general downtown rowdiness, most of the local police expect it and won't harass each and every drunken college student—they'd never get any sleep if they did. However, if you're caught being especially rowdy and too inebriated for your own good, you will be taken in. Being cited for underage drinking or providing to minors means a hefty fine and a required class about the dangers of alcohol. Although Penn State is a party school, this doesn't mean the students have free license to do whatever they want; the town does take public disturbances and lawbreaking very seriously, and police are constantly on patrol during the weekends and holidays.

B-

The College Prowler® Grade on

Campus
Strictness: B-

A high Campus Strictness grade implies an overall lenient atmosphere; police and RAs are fairly tolerant, and the administration's rules are flexible.

Parking

The Lowdown On...
Parking

Approximate Parking Permit Cost:

Residence Hall: $275 per semester, $520 per year

Off Campus: $145 per semester, $260 per year

Student Parking Lot?

There are several around the perimeter of campus, depending on residency.

Freshmen Allowed to Park?

No

Common Parking Tickets:

Expired Meter: $11

Wrong Area: $11

No Parking Zone: $15

Reserved Space: $15

Handicapped Zone: $50

Parking Permits:

Green – Residence
Hall storage

Red – Commuter

Blue – Grad Circle and
Eastview Terrace

Purple – Off-Campus Storage

Yellow – Evening and
Weekend

Black – Motorcycle

Parking Requirements:

Students are required to have
28 credits completed before
they qualify for a parking
permit. All vehicles must be
registered before the first day
of classes each semester, or
one day after your arrival on
campus (if you come after the
semester has started).

Did You Know?

Best Place to Find a Parking Spot:

Residence halls have small, reserved (permit) lots for
students, but these are **generally packed**. Parking
on the outer edges of campus is your best bet,
though even this is unreliable at best.

Good Luck Getting a Parking Spot Here!

Anywhere that is remotely convenient. Most on-campus lots
are reserved for faculty and staff, and non-permit lots are
nearly always full.

Students Speak Out On...
Parking

"If you could find a place to park a skateboard on campus, I'd be impressed. They ticket people for just thinking of parking on campus. Walk or ride the campus loop service."

Q "**Parking is horrible on campus**. With over 40,000 students, there are less than 3,000 parking spots. It is not worth it to bring a car up to school."

Q "Okay, parking is not so cool. I do not have a car at school because it is expensive to park, sometimes hard to find a spot, and **it's very easy to get a ticket**."

Q "Parking is the biggest pain on campus. Not only is there little student parking, but it is also only located in one area: by East Halls. **The University does everything it can to screw student drivers** by providing little parking and always trying to nail them with tickets."

Q "**If you live in the dorms, parking sucks**, and it's not getting much better. It's all in one area, but it's far away from most of the campus. It's actually real close to the freshmen dorms, but you can't have a car unless you have 28 credits or more, or you have some other really good reason. Parking off campus can be a hassle and is sometimes expensive unless you have a good connection with someone."

Q "**Freshmen aren't allowed to have cars**. Parking on campus is available, but you have to be willing to pay for a permit. I won't be bringing a car, but it's not because of the additional cost. What's great about the University Park campus is the convenience of everything. There are always buses running, and the downtown area is so cool. The town fits the needs of the school, and the school is in concert with the town. It's awesome."

Q "**Parking is horrible**. It's worse than NYC and Washington DC combined."

Q "Parking sucks at PSU! If you have a parking pass, **good luck finding a spot that is within a mile of your quarters**. If you don't have a parking pass, good luck finding an open meter, and prepare to be ticketed."

Q "Parking is bad. One of the over-reaching goals of the administration is to **eliminate on-campus driving and parking**, so you can probably imagine what it would be like."

Q "**Ha! There is no parking here**. At least not close enough that you would hike to your car unless you really need it. Freshmen cannot even have cars on campus."

The College Prowler Take On...
Parking

Parking is one of students' biggest complaints and arguably the most ignored. Despite construction on campus, no new lots are being built, and existing lots are all located on the outskirts of campus. Parking has also gotten more expensive over the last few years. For freshmen, there's no reason to worry about parking. Students can't bring a car until after their first year. Many students feel that it's easier to rely on walking and public transportation, rather than dealing with cost and hard-to-find parking spaces. State College isn't difficult to navigate without a vehicle. Everything you need in town is within walking distance, and there is public transportation that goes directly to the major shopping areas across town.

Given the largeness of central Pennsylvania, having your own car gives students the opportunity to explore rustic state parks and neighboring towns on weekends. If you want to get the most out of the local area, having a car is something to consider in your later years at the University. This is especially true if you end up living off campus, because parking around most apartments and townhouses is much better. Downtown State College has metered parking, so be sure to have plenty of quarters handy. In addition to these areas, there are two municipal parking garages (off Pugh and Fraser Streets) that are convenient and generally have space available—the exception, of course, being football weekends. Most metered lots aren't checked on Sundays, and during the holiday season, the State College borough offers free garage parking and increased shuttle service.

The College Prowler® Grade on

Parking: D

A high grade in this section indicates that parking is both available and affordable, and that parking enforcement isn't overly severe.

Transportation

The Lowdown On...
Transportation

Ways to Get Around Town:

On Campus
Bus
Bicycle
The Campus Loop
The Link
Rollerblades
Skateboard
The Town Loop

Public Transportation
CATA buses, for local travel
www.catabus.com

Taxi Cabs
Taxis are a popular way for kids to be chauffeured to or from parties, keeping them from getting behind the wheel themselves. If you're planning to party, keep these numbers handy like you would a coupon for free beer.

Centre County Taxi For Less
2017 N. Atherton St.
(814) 238-7900

Taxi by Handy Delivery
2197 High Tech Rd.
(814) 353-6001

→

Car Rentals

Avis
national (800) 778-5519;
local (814) 237-9750
www.avis.com

Hertz
national (800) 654-3131;
local (814) 237-1728
www.hertz.com

National
national (800) 227-7368;
local (814) 237-1771
www.nationalcar.com

Ways to Get Out of Town:

Airports

University Park Airport
2535 Fox Hill Rd.
(814) 865-5511

Bellefonte Airport
612 Buffalo Run Rd., Bellefonte
(814) 355-7407

The University Park airport is quite tiny, but convenient. It is located about 4 miles from campus. If you know how to fly (or have friends who do), there is also an airport in Bellefonte (about 8 miles away) for personal airplanes.

Airlines Serving State College

Northwest Airlink
(800) 225-2525

United Airlines
(800) 241-6522

US Airways Express
(800) 428-4322

Bus

There is a bus station right on campus which offers really cheap, easy, and frequent trips to nearby cities, such as Philly, Pittsburgh, Baltimore, DC, and NYC. Stop in for a full schedule to keep in your dorm room, if ever you need to leave State College in a hurry.

Fullington Trailways
152 N. Atherton St.
(814) 238-1100

Greyhound Bus Lines
152 N. Atherton St.
(814) 238-7971

Travel Agents

Nittany Travel
(814) 238-2722
www.nittanytravel.com

Students Speak Out On...
Transportation

> **"The Loop, the Link, and the other CATA buses will take you where you want to go."**

Q "Public transportation is pretty decent, although if you are on campus, **there isn't much of a need for it**. You only need the bus if you live in far, off-campus apartments. Even then, you'll probably know someone with a car."

Q "Public transportation, like the campus buses, run almost every 10 minutes and they really only go around campus, so **it's easy to find a stop close to your destination**."

Q "**Public transportation is the key**. The Loop is free and has two circular (one clockwise, one counter clockwise) routes around the campus and the main streets downtown. All lazy kids can catch the Loop and get dropped off near their classes easily. Other buses that go out to the shopping mall, Wal-Mart, and Sam's Club are only a buck each way—very affordable."

Q "PSU is a big campus. **Free bus service** runs from approximately 7 a.m. to 3 a.m. on campus. And you can catch the bus to the Nittany Mall or to Bellefonte for only a buck."

Q "The town and campus buses are free. **Other area buses sometimes charge $1** depending on which ones you need (Wal-Mart, Kmart, Barnes and Nobles, the mall, or apartments that are far)."

Q "The Town and Campus Loops are **the easiest and cheapest** way to get around town."

Q "**Transportation is better during the school year**. It's not so good during the summer."

Q "The Loop is free and takes you all around campus and downtown. **The buses never seem to come as often as you would like** and are usually crowded by the time they arrive—especially during the winter. They've fixed the problem lately by having 'free zones' on the regular pay buses as well. The pay buses go all over and have pretty decent schedules, although some stop running a little early, I think."

Q "Town is so close to campus **you don't really need public transportation**. The Loop is a wonderful thing, especially when it's 10 degrees out and you need to go across campus! If you don't have a car, the buses are good to get out to the mall or the grocery store, too."

The College Prowler Take On...
Transportation

The availability of public transportation around the Penn State area makes up for the terrible parking situation. The Campus Loop and Town Loop are area buses that run in opposite directions pretty much all day and late into the night. There are numerous stops throughout campus and downtown. Buses are scheduled to arrive every 8 minutes; the most you should ever have to wait will be about 15 minutes. Always allow extra time if you're depending on public transit, especially during the cold months when the buses are crowded. However, the transit authority has recently added newer lines that are "fare-free" on campus in an effort to make them less crowded. Buses also run throughout State College, including off-campus housing areas.

Many landlords provide free bus passes to students, although regular fare is only a dollar. Every major store in the area is accessible via public transit, so you'll have no problem shopping or spending an evening away from downtown. Off-campus buses go to shopping areas such as Atherton Street's Wal-Mart and Best Buy plazas, and the Nittany Mall on College Avenue. If you feel like exploring the area, the historic towns of Bellefonte and Boalsburg are also on this line. For getting out of town, the University Park Airport and bus station are convenient. The airport is a quick cab ride from campus, and the bus station is within reasonable walking distance. Flying is not always cheap, but at least the planes out of State College tend to run on time. Buses travel across the nation and are an inexpensive alternative to putting miles on your car. Just don't expect to get much sleep.

B-

The College Prowler® Grade on

Transportation: B-

A high grade for Transportation indicates that campus buses, public buses, cabs, and rental cars are readily-available and affordable. Other determining factors include proximity to an airport and the necessity of transportation.

Weather

The Lowdown On...
Weather

Average Temperature:		Average Precipitation:	
Fall:	40°F	Fall:	12.17 in.
Winter:	26°F	Winter:	10.45 in.
Spring:	55°F	Spring:	11.72 in.
Summer:	71°F	Summer:	11.09 in.

Students Speak Out On...
Weather

> **"It's not as bad as you would expect. It does definitely get cold in the winter, but it is manageable because of public transportation. It's real nice in the spring and fall."**

Q "The fall is awesome—the trees and grass leave such a brisk feeling in the air. **It can be rough to get motivated in the winter** since getting to class can be quite a hike. And the spring's usually gloomy until the last month and then it's beautiful and relaxing."

Q "**The weather? Somebody please shoot me**. The winters are frigid with tons of snow. A kid that grew up in State College once told me that State College gets the most rain next to Seattle; I believe it—it's absolutely miserable at times."

Q "Centre County weather is winter and summer weather. During the school year, it's about three months of summer and then seven of winter. **The sun can be a stranger in the winter**."

Q "It can get cold here in the winter. However, **fall is absolutely beautiful**, especially spending Saturday at the football stadium for great JoePa football. There were times we had 70 degrees in February, but there were also times we had 30-degree temps in April. The weather can change fast. Wind chills can be a factor, as some parts of campus are windy when it's cold. It generally warms up at the end of the semester, and for the last two or three weeks, you'll see lots of people sun tanning."

Q "We're stuck in a valley surrounded by mountains where all the clouds get stuck. So we rarely see the sun, and it rains a lot. **Bring a jacket**."

Q "**It's overcast and cold for most of the year**. I haven't seen the sun for four months straight. It snowed for eight months this year."

Q "Since we're in a valley (Happy Valley), it tends to rain and be overcast a lot. **Winters get pretty cold and snowy**."

Q "**Warm clothes are a necessity**. You will be wearing more winter items than summer."

Q "Sometime in October, the wind starts blowing and doesn't stop until about April or May. When April rolls around, it will be about 90 degrees one day, then 10 degrees the next. Needless to say, **bring a variety of clothing and a heavy coat**."

Q "**The weather is nuts here**. It can be sunny and warm one day, and snowing the next. No, wait, I mean it can do all that in one day. In general, it is cold. 'Spring' semester it is freezing and snowing, until finals week when it gets warm just when you should be inside studying. Any day that parents come up, like for football games and parent's weekend, it is inevitably beautiful and warm."

The College Prowler Take On...
Weather

You'll find a large range of opinion about the weather in State College. Pennsylvania weather is a lesson in extremes. Winter is a long, cold season, but it's not necessarily something to worry about. The months between October and April are often cold and overcast, and the area does get a fair share of lake-effect snow. If you're coming from farther north, weather will be noticeably milder during a normal season. The town usually shuts down at least twice a year to clean up after large snowstorms. This can mean a nice break from class, a chance for skiing and snowball fights, or a cabin-fever-inducing wasteland. It all depends on how you look at it.

Spring and autumn are particularly beautiful in Central Pennsylvania. The entire region is surrounded by forests and mountains, and there is a lot of open country if you appreciate natural landscapes. During the summer, if you're still around, it can get very hot—upwards of 90 degrees, with high humidity. This huge variation in climate means that you'll want to be prepared for every type of weather. While climate might not be a make-or-break factor in choosing a college, it's definitely a something to consider—especially when you're packing or buying clothes to accommodate sub-zero to sub-tropical temperatures.

The College Prowler® Grade on

Weather: C

A high Weather grade designates that temperatures are mild and rarely reach extremes, that the campus tends to be sunny rather than rainy, and that weather is fairly consistent rather than unpredictable.

Report Card Summary

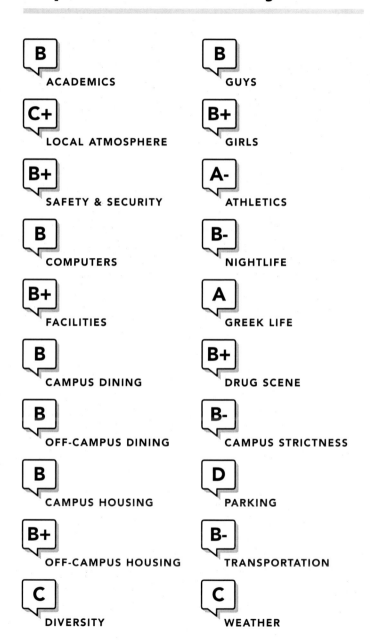

B ACADEMICS

C+ LOCAL ATMOSPHERE

B+ SAFETY & SECURITY

B COMPUTERS

B+ FACILITIES

B CAMPUS DINING

B OFF-CAMPUS DINING

B CAMPUS HOUSING

B+ OFF-CAMPUS HOUSING

C DIVERSITY

B GUYS

B+ GIRLS

A- ATHLETICS

B- NIGHTLIFE

A GREEK LIFE

B+ DRUG SCENE

B- CAMPUS STRICTNESS

D PARKING

B- TRANSPORTATION

C WEATHER

Overall Experience

Students Speak Out On...
Overall Experience

{ **"My experience in school has been phenomenal. I can't ask for more. I have everything I need."**

"I love Penn State. I wish to be nowhere else. The atmosphere is relaxed, and it is a **nationally-recognized Big Ten school**. There are lots of ways to get involved in different organizations, and the school spirit is tremendous."

"**I have loved my time at PSU**, and there is no other school I would rather attend. I have made so many friends there and had such a great time that I wish I could go for another four years."

Q "I would never dream about going anywhere else. **This has been the best three years and counting of my life**, so far. I've learned more and experienced more than I would have ever dreamed. Penn State was the best decision I've made in my life."

Q "Penn State has something for everyone, I think. Penn State is alright. Try to get a car if you can because it gets boring, but that can happen anywhere. I mean after living somewhere for a while, you do everything and then start looking for new options. **Overall, this school is great, and the best part is the football games**. Even if you don't like the sport, the games are fun, and almost every student has tons of spirit."

Q "I graduated from PSU last May and had a wonderful experience there. **It was the best four years of my life**! The campus has so much to offer and many activities to get involved in. It definitely has a reputation of a 'drinking town,' and there is plenty of that, but if you aren't into partying, there are so many other options."

Q "**Basically, there are two things that govern PSU: drinking and football**. There are always parties going on, tons of frats and sororities, and when you do turn 21 or obtain a fake ID, there are plenty of bars. School is pretty challenging, though. Depending on how well you can retain information, whether you like to go to class or not, and your study habits, it's not impossible to receive an 'A,' but it takes a good bit of work.

Q "I have had a splendid time at school because of the people I've met and the subjects I've studied. I could've gone somewhere else, but I don't regret coming here. After a while, **you do start to grow attached to this place and the people**. I'm actually surprised there isn't a wall around campus. All in all, I did love my time here."

Q **"It's amazing here**! I wouldn't trade my experience here for the world. The best part of it was the people I've met and the personal growth I've gained from being on my own. PSU is s a fun place and a challenging academic institution. I'm glad I'm here."

Q "Overall, **this school is top-notch**. I can go anywhere and tell people that I go to PSU and they congratulate me about choosing such a fine institution. You can get very far after PSU."

Q "I can't say I've had the best experience at school, but I can't imagine having had a better time anywhere else. For the people I've met, the classes I've taken, and all the money I've spent, **I think Penn State is a pretty good place to be**."

Q "Overall, my experience here is good. I never wanted to transfer to another school. I cursed the weather and the foreign teaching assistants many times, as well as the science department's system for curving grades. But **you will meet someone new everyday**, have wonderful random experiences, and get a good education. WE ARE . . . PENN STATE."

The College Prowler Take On...
Overall Experience

Despite common reservations about the location and climate, most Penn State students are fiercely loyal to their alma mater. Penn State boasts one of the largest alumni populations in the United States; graduates are proud of their degrees, and employers recognize the University's name immediately. Although the campus is located in a very rural area, school is technologically up-to-date and on the cutting-edge of current research.

Aside from academics, PSU is also known for its social scene, especially in relation to sports and parties. Nittany Lion football—home of the 2006 Orange Bowl Champions—is a national draw and a point of pride for both the University and the town of State College. For anyone interested in playing or watching varsity sports, PSU is a top choice. Penn State has also been ranked highly by many polls and "party school" surveys as one of the top party schools in the nation. While it certainly isn't the wildest town, these rankings are definitely accurate. The small-town setting and large-school atmosphere makes for little else in the way of entertainment, so it can be hard to avoid encountering the party scene during your time as a student. Still, the mix of work and leisure seems to work well for most of the student body, and academic standards at Penn State remain relatively high. It's easy to spend four years at Penn State as an ever-serious student, focused completely on whatever you choose to study. With so many opportunities to relax nearby, balance and moderation are some of the best skills to learn from your four years in college.

The Inside Scoop

The Lowdown On...
The Inside Scoop

Penn State Slang:

Know the slang, know the school. The following is a list of things you really need to know before coming to PSU. The more of these words you know, the better off you'll be.

BJC – The Bryce Jordan Center, home of PSU basketball and numerous shows and events.

Chipped ham/beef – Thinly sliced deli meat.

"The College" (pronounced "caw-ledg") – Local drawl/slang for State College.

The HUB – The Hetzel Union Building, the student center on campus.

Pop – Soda, according to about half the state.

"The Projects" – An affectionate term for East Halls, the freshmen dorms.

ResCom – Residential Computing, the people you want to know if you have any computer problems, in student labs or with your personal computer.

JoePa – Joe Paterno, the famous Nittany Lion football coach.

The Wall – The area along College Ave., by the University gate; a daily hangout for bored students and odd townies.

Things I Wish I Knew Before Coming to Penn State

- There is constant construction on campus.
- It is very, very far to the nearest urban area.
- Rural life isn't always what it's made out to be.
- Intro classes are best done through AP credits; or used as nap time.
- For those from warmer climates, it snows a lot.
- For those from colder climates, it snows a lot.

Tips to Succeed at Penn State

- The fact that partying at PSU is ever-pervasive doesn't mean you have to always be involved in order to be cool. There's bound to be parties happening at least five nights a week. College will be your first chance to party every night without anyone to watch over you. Try to work out a schedule that allows you to party without burning yourself out. Early on, things seem really easy, but this will definitely change as time goes on.

- Drink responsibly. It seems cliché, but when you spend enough time around people who don't, you start to realize just how important it is.

- Read the *Collegian* to keep updated and involved with what's going on at school. Also, keep up with the *Weekender* (Fridays in the CDT) so you'll know what's going on in the area—though there isn't much of it, cool stuff does come around pretty frequently.

- Visit the Daily Jolt (*http://psu.dailyjolt.com*) for everything from national news, procrastination tools, club postings, candid professor quotes, and dinner menus.

Must-See Things at Penn State

These are some of the many sights that every student must visit at least once during their stay on campus:

A football game – Even if you hate sports, there is something amazing about seeing 100,000 people gathered in one place cheering for the same team.

The JoePa Statue – A much more recent addition to the monstrous stadium, it is a bronze statue of Joe Paterno, the famous PSU football coach who, although in his seventies, is still energetically leading the Lions to victory. Whether or not you care about football, Paterno is a likeable figure and an asset to the school.

The Lion Shrine – A larger-than-life sculpture of the school mascot, which was presented to the school in the 1940s. It's standard to have your photo taken here by your family when you first arrive on campus, and of course, in your graduation robes.

Old Main – The first building on the Penn State campus in 1855, it was essentially the Penn State campus. It was both dormitory and classroom to the students; now it houses President Spanier and his administration. Though the modern version isn't exactly original (it was rebuilt in 1930), it retains its historic significance.

The Palmer Art Museum – A small but respectable art museum housing everything from ancient Roman coins to modern, abstract blown glass. The building itself was designed by famous architect Charles Moore.

Penn State Urban Legends

"Nittany" is named for Native American Princess Nita-nee, a former inhabitant of the region. Historically, Princess Nita-nee never existed; however, the name is derived from a Native American term meaning "single mountain."

Sororities aren't allowed houses because, under State College law, a house with 16 or more women living together is considered a brothel. This is also false: sorority houses did exist on campus until the 1950s, when sororities relocated to newly-available residence hall housing. State College zoning law makes no distinction between fraternity and sorority houses.

The campus loop arrives every eight minutes. Okay, so this technically isn't an "urban legend," but when you're standing in sub-zero temperatures long enough, you will probably start to vehemently debate it.

The ghost of an actress who died in Schwab Auditorium still haunts it. Whether this is true or not, some backstage areas of Schwab are definitely creepy!

Mrs. Atherton, the wife of former PSU President Atherton (1882–1906), haunts Old Botany, so she can watch over her husband's grave. (Ghost hunting, anyone?)

The sun-dial on the Old Main Lawn marks the geographic center of Pennsylvania. (False—and who comes up with this stuff, anyway?) The sun dial was a gift from the class of 1915, and holds no more significance than historic value.

School Spirit

School spirit at Penn State is stronger than most schools you can name. Nittany Lion Pride is taken very seriously, as is respect for coach Joe Paterno and the famed Lion Shrine. To help you acclimate to the Lion vibe, there are about four stores downtown that sell large quantities of Penn State clothing and souvenirs. On campus, the Penn State Bookstore has an enormous selection of Penn State clothing and collectibles, though you will pay top dollar there. The Family Clothesline, downtown, is known for having the best selection and prices.

Traditions

Not knowing the words to the Alma Mater is probably the greatest Penn State tradition. Students typically know the general tune, but sing "I don't know the words to this song" instead of any actual lyrics.

The Mifflin Streak—every year, the students of Mifflin Hall streak across campus. No one quite knows why, but it is a long-standing tradition.

Every year, PSU's Interfraternity Council sponsors THON, a 48-hour dance marathon intended to raise money for charity. One year, Penn State students raised $3,547,716 for the Four-Diamonds Fund.

Finding a Job or Internship

The Lowdown On...
Finding a Job or Internship

1 in every 720 people in the U.S. is a Penn State graduate. This means that alumni are present in just about every field imaginable. This connection is often a great way to get your foot in the door. Career Services used to be located in the top couple floors of the Boucke Building. Over the past few years, Penn State has built a beautiful new building along Bigler Avenue dedicated solely to helping students find the right major, internship, job, and career. The Career Center offers frequent workshops and recruiting fairs. By far, the easiest way to access this information is online, at the Career Center's Web site.

Advice

Take advantage of the frequent career fairs held on campus, especially if you are interested in business or computers. Almost 1,000 companies converge at these fairs to find new recruits, enabling many students to graduate with career plans already in place.

Career Center Resources & Services

www.sa.psu.edu/career

Grads Who Enter the Job Market Within

6 months: 57%
1 Year: N/A

Firms that Most Frequently Hire Grads

Accenture, Black and Decker, Deloitte Consulting, DuPont, Exxon Mobil, Ferguson, Foot Locker, Inc., General Electric, IBM, Johnson & Johnson, Liberty Mutual, Lockheed Martin, Lutron Electronics, Merck & Co., Microsoft, Northrop Grumman, Newell Rubbermaid, NVR Ryan Homes, The Pepsi Bottling Group, PPG, Schlumberger Technology Corp., Shell, Target, US Gypsum, Westinghouse

Alumni

The Lowdown On...
Alumni

Web Site:
www.alumni.psu.edu

E-Mail:
kbarron@psu.edu

Office:
Hintz Family Alumni Center
University Park, PA 16802
(800) 548-LION

Services Available:
Alumni directory online
Alumni Outreach
Career services
E-Mail forwarding
Financial services
Home & auto insurance
License plates
Life and medical insurance
Penn State travel program

➜

Alumni Services for Students:

FastStart – A mentoring program to help freshmen give their college careers a running start.

LionLink – A networking service keeping Penn State students and alumni in contact for everything from mentoring to making job connections.

Programs Supported:

Admissions

Alumni Fellows – Award presented to an alumnus/a who, as a leader in his or her field, is invited back to campus by the President to interact with the current community.

Lion Ambassadors – Students who represent Penn State in public forums.

Networking and Mentoring

Parents and Families Day

Recognition – A program designed to recognize Penn Staters for outstanding community service and academic achievement.

Reunions and Homecoming

Major Alumni Events

National Service Week – One week of the year, alumni commit themselves to helping out and providing various community activities.

Social Gatherings – Happy hours, luncheons, picnics, cruises, and pep rallies during football season are held all over the country throughout the year to keep Penn State pride going in the extended community.

Alumni Publications

Penn Stater Magazine

The Football Letter

College or Campus Society Publications

Did You Know?

Famous PSU Alums

Charles Bierbauer – Journalist, news anchor

Carmen Finestra – Actress

Jonathan Frakes – Actor

Roosevelt Grier – Football star, actor

Franco Harris – Football star

Student Organizations

For a complete, up-to-date listing of all campus organizations, see: *http://clubs.psu.edu.*

Academic

AAUW

Accounting Club

Actuarial Science Club

Adult Learners of Penn State

Advertising Club

Agricultural and Extension Education Graduate Student Association

Agricultural Systems Management Club

Agriculture Student Council

Agronomy Club

Alpha Epsilon

Alpha Epsilon Delta

Alpha Kappa Psi

Alpha Pi Mu

American Ceramic Society

American College of Healthcare Executives

American Concrete Institute

American Fisheries Society

American Institute of Chemical Engineers

American Institute of Aeronautics & Astronautics

American Nuclear Society

American Society for Microbiology

American Society of Civil Engineers

American Society of Mechanical Engineers

American Water Resources Association

Architectural Engineering Graduate Student Association

Architectural Student Society

Art Education Graduate Students Club

Arts and Architecture Undergraduate Student Council

ASAE

ASHRAE

Association for Computing Machinery

Association for Educated Banking

Association of Collegiate Entrepreneurs

Astronomy Club

Audio Engineering Society

Beta Alpha Psi

Beta Gamma Sigma

Biochemistry Society

Biology Club

Biomedical Engineering Society

Block and Bridle Club

Business Administration Student Council

Business and Society House

Business Roundtable

Chi Epsilon Pi

Chi Sigma Iota Honor Society

Club Managers Association of America

Coaly Society

College of Communications Student Council

College of Education Graduate Student Association

College Student Personnel Association

Collegiate FFA

Computer Science and Engineering Graduate Student Council

Dairy Science Club

Delta Sigma Pi

Design Build Institute of America

Division of Undergraduate Studies Student Council

Earth and Mineral Science Student Council

Eberly College Science Student Council

Economics Association

Education Student Council

Emergency Medical Services Association

Energy, Environmental, and Mineral Economics Society

Engineering Graduate Student Council

Engineering Leadership Development Unlimited

Engineering Undergraduate Student Council

Engineers Without Frontiers

Environmental Economics Club

Environmental Engineering Society

Environmental Society

Eta Sigma Delta

Finance Club

Food Science Club

Forest Products Society

Gamma Iota Sigma

Gamma Theta Upsilon

Geological Sciences Club

Gerontology Outreach Volunteers

Global AIDS Initiative

Graduate Women in Science

HEAL

Health and Human Development Honor Society

Health and Human Development Undergraduate
Student Council

Health and Physical Education Teachers Club

Health Policy & Administration Club

Horticulture Club

Hotel and Restaurant Society

Hotel Sales and Marketing Association

Human Factors and Ergonomics Society

Illuminating Engineering Society

Industrial Engineering Graduate Association

Industrial Health and Safety Society

Information Systems Association

INFORMS (Institute for Ops. Research & the Mgmt. Sci.)

Institute of Transportation Engineers

Intelligent Transportation Society of America

International Business Association

Investment Association

Kappa Theta Epsilon

Kinesiology Club

Kinesiology Graduate Student Association

Landscape Architecture Student Society

Liberal Arts Undergraduate Council

Logistics Association

Marine Science Society

Marketing Association

Materials Research Society

Math Club

Mechanical and Nuclear Engineering Graduate Student Council

Mining Society

Minorities in Agriculture & Natural Resources

Minorities in Science and Technology

Minority MBA Association

Mu Sigma Upsilon

National Agri-Marketing Association

National Association of Black Accountants

National Hispanic Business Association

National Society of Black Engineers

National Society of Minorities in Hospitality

Nittany Chemical Society

Nutrition Graduate Student Association

Omega Chi Epsilon

Phi Beta Lambda

Phi Chi Theta

Phi Gamma Nu

Philosophy Club

Pi Alpha Xi

Pi Lambda Theta

Poultry Science Club

Pre-Dental Society

Pre-Physical Therapy Club

Pre-Vet Club

Professional Management Association

Real Estate Club

Recreations and Parks Society

SAP Student Interest Group

Schreyer Honors College Student Council

Science Lions

Sigma Alpha

Sigma Gamma Tau

Sigma Iota Epsilon

Sigma Phi Omega

Smeal PHD Association

Smeal Student Mentors

Society for Biobehavioral Health

Society for Human Resource Management

Society of Automotive Engineers

Society of Engineering Science

Society of Environmental Systems Engineers

Society of Labor and Industrial Relations

Society of Physics Students
Society of Medical Sciences
Society of Women Engineers
Student Health Advisory Board
Student National Medical Association
Student Nurses Association
Student Nutrition Association
Student Pennsylvania State Education Association
Student Society of Architectural Engineers
Student Structural Engineers Association
Students of Partnership for Achieving Construction Exc.
Turf Grass Club
Underdogs
Undergraduate Statistics Club
Wildlife Society
Women in Business
Women's Studies Graduate Organization
Xi Sigma Pi

Athletic and Recreational
Aikido Club
Archery Club
Badminton Club
Ballroom Dance Club
Barbell Club
Baseball Club
Billiards Club
Blue Crew
Bowling Club
Boxing Club
Chess Team
Crew Club
Cricket Club
Cycling Club

Dance Team

East Halls Gym

Equestrian Team

Fencing Club

Field Hockey Club

Floor Hockey Association

Fly Fishing Club

Gaming Association

Golf Club

Gymnastics Club

Hockey Management Association

Ice Lions

Indoor Winter Guard

International Soccer Club

Judo Club

Juggling Club

Jung Sim Do Martial Arts Club

Karate Club

Korean Karate Club

Martial Arts Group

Men's Lacrosse Club

Nittany Divers Scuba Club

Nittany Grotto Club

Nittany Lion Racquetball Club

Outing Club Main Division

Outing Club Whitewater Division

Paintball Association

Pollock Fitness Center

Power Volleyball Club

Powerlifting Club

Pro Wrestling Club

Professional Golf Management

Quantum Jujitsu

Rifle Team Club

Road Runners

Roller Hockey Club

Rugby Football Club

Sailing Club

Select Soccer

Shotokan Karate-do

Ski Team

Snowboard Team

Soaring Club

Soccer Club

Squash Club

Student Athlete Advisory Board

Student Athlete Trainers Club

Student Skating Club

Swing Dancing Club

Synchronized Swimming

Table Tennis Club

Tae Kwon Do Club

Tae Kwon Do Players Team

Tennis Club

Triathlon Club

Ultimate Frisbee Club

Water Polo Club

Water Ski Club

Women's Club Basketball

Women's Club Fastpitch Softball Team

Women's Ice Hockey Team

Women's Lacrosse Club

Women's Rugby Football Club

Women's Soccer Club

Wrestling

Humanities and Political Organizations

Alliance for Animal Rights

Alpha Kappa Delta

Alpha Phi Sigma

American Civil Liberties Union

Americanists

Amnesty International

Anthropology Graduate Student Association

Anthropology Society

Campus Greens

College Democrats

College Libertarians

College Republicans

Eta Sigma Phi

Feminist Majority Leadership Alliance

Gamma Sigma Sigma

Graduate Philosophy Club

History Roundtable

Independent Women's Club

Iota Iota Iota

Justice Association

Kappa Omicron Nu

League of United Latin American Citizens (LULAC)

Mock Trial Association

Model United Nations

Objectivist Club

Optimist Club

Phi Alpha Theta

Phi Upsilon Omicron

Political Science Society

Pro-Choice

Psi Chi

Students and Youth Against Racism

Students for Free Tibet

Students For Life
Students for the Responsible Use of Animals
Turkish Association for Secularism & Kemalism
Undergraduate Law Society
Veteran's Organization (PSUVO)
Womyn's Concerns
Young Americans for Freedom

International and Multicultural
African Students Association
Allies
American Indian Tribal Alliance
Arab Union Society
Asian Pacific American Coalition
Association for India's Development
Black Caucus
Black Graduate Student Association
Cambodian Student Coalition
Caribbean Student Association
Chinese Friendship Association
Coalition of Lesbian, Gay, Bisexual & Transgendered
Graduate Students
European Student Club
Filipino Association
French Club
French Graduate Organization
Friends of Brazil
German Club
Hawaii Club
Hellenic Society
Hong Kong Student Association
Indian Graduate Student Association
Indian Student Association
Indonesian Student Association

International Language Interest House
International Student Council
International Students' Social Club
Iranian Student Association
Irish Student Organization
Israeli Student Association (PISA)
Italian Club
Japanese Friendship Association
Japanese-American Association
Korean Students Association
Korean Undergraduate Student Association
Kuwaiti Students Association
Lambda Student Alliance
Latin American Students Association
Latino Caucus
Multicultural Business Society
NAACP
Pakistan Student Association
Project Haiti Student Association
Puerto Rican Student Association
Punjabi Student Organization
Sigma Chi Alpha
Sigma Iota Alpha
Singapore Students Association
Society of Hispanic Professional Engineers
Spanish Club
Spanish, Italian, and Portuguese Student Organization
Student Minority Advisory and Recruitment Team
Taiwanese American Student Association
Taiwanese Student Association
Thai Student Group
Turkish Student Association
Vietnamese Student Association

Media, Technology and Publications

Association of Journalists for Diversity
College Club Nittany Lions
Digital: Media Group
E-Commerce
Forensics Council
Graduate Students in Communication
IEEE Computer Society
Information Technology Club (ITC)
IST Undergraduate Student Government
La Vie
Linux Users Group
Mars Society
National Association of Minorities in Communication
National Student Speech Language Hearing Association
Phroth
Problem Child Literary Magazine
Public Relations Student Society
Radio-Television News Directors Association
Sign Language Organization
Society of Professional Journalists
Speak Up
Student Television Society
The *Scoop*
WEHR-FM (93.7 FM)
WKPS Radio FM-91
Women in Cable and Telecommunications
Women in Information Sciences and Technology
Writer's Kiosk

Music and Performance

Anime/Manga Organization
Art of Soul - African American Theater Company
ASTA w/ NSOA

Blue Band

Collegiate Music Educators National Conference

Concert Choir

Delta Omicron

Essence of Joy

Glee Club

Indoor Drumline

Intercollegiate Speech Team

International Association of Jazz Educators

International Dance Ensemble

Jazz Club

Monster Squad

Monty Python Society

Mu Phi Epsilon

No Refund Theatre

NOMMO

None of the Above (NOTA)

Orchesis Dance Company

Oriana Singers

Pennsylvania Art Education Association

Performing Magicians

Phi Mu Alpha Sinfonia

Recording Engineering Collaboration

Savoir Faire

Screenwriting Organization

Singing Lions

State College Interactive Theatre Society

Student Film Organization

Synergy

Tapestry

The Next Generation

Thespians

Trombone Choir

United Soul Ensemble Gospel Choir

University Choir
US Institute of Theatre Technology (USITT)
Vole (Ballet)
Women's Chorale

Religious and Spiritual
Alliance Christian Fellowship
Antioch Campus Ministry
Asian American Christian Fellowship
Bahai Club
Campus Ambassadors
Campus Bible Fellowship
Campus Crusade For Christ
Chabad
Chi Alpha Christian Fellowship
Chinese Buddhism Study Association
Chinese Student, Scholar, and Family Ministries
Christian Grads
Christian Science Organization
Christian Student Fellowship
Christians in Action
Episcopal Student Association
Falun Dafa
Fresh Look Adventist Fellowship
Fusion
Hillel
Infuse
International Christian Fellowship
JADE (Jewish, Awareness, Diversity, and Education)
Kappa Phi
Korean Buddhism Organization
Korean Students for Christ
Latter Day Saints Student Association
Living Stones Christian Fellowship

Lutheran Student Community

Muslim Student Association

Navigators

New Life Student Fellowship

Newman Catholic Student Association

Nittany Lions for Christ

Organization of Hindu Minds

Origins Club

Orthodox Christian Fellowship

Pax Christi

Reformed University Fellowship

Silent Praise

Silver Circle

Unitarian Universalist Students

United Campus Ministry

Unity Christian Campus Ministry

Wesley Student Fellowship

Young Life Leadership Initiative

Service, Leadership, and Honors

Adopt a School

Alpha Phi Omega

Alternative Spring Break Club

Best Buddies

Blue and White Society

Circle K

Collegians Helping Aid Rescue Missions (CHARM)

Collegiate 4-H Club

Eco Action

Fraternal Order of Auxiliary Officers

Golden Key International Honour Society

Habitat for Humanity

Helping Across the Community

Mortar Board

National Society of Collegiate Scholars
Omicron Delta Kappa
Parmi Nous Society
Phi Eta Sigma
Rotaract Club
Skull and Bones Society
Special Olympics Club
Student Council for Exceptional Children
Student Red Cross Club
Student United Way
Theta Alpha Pi
Theta Kappa Pi

Special Interest
Amateur Radio Club
American Helicopter Society
Arnold Air Society
Asylum
Future Marine Officers Association
Honor Guard Booster Club
House Blend
Language Acquisition Graduate Organization
Lions Performance Auto Club
Meditation Community
Men Stopping Rape
Miss Penn State Scholarship Organization
Model Railroad
Motorcycle Club
Mud Club
National Association of Home Builders
National Residence Hall Honorary
Operation Smile
Paranormal Research Society

Parrothead Club

Peer Mediators

Photography Society

Quiz Bowl

Rescue Childhood

Russian Society

Science Fiction Society

Student Fire Safety Commission

Student Parent Organization

Supporting Women in Geography (SWIG)

Vedic Society

Walt Disney World Alumni Association

Woodsmen Team

Yan Xin Qigong Club

Yoga and Meditation Society

Student Government

Association of Residence Hall Students

Council of Commonwealth Student Governments

East Halls Residence Association

Graduate Student Association

Interfraternity Council

Multicultural Greek Council (MGC)

National Panhellenic Council (NPHC)

North Halls Association of Students

Panhellenic Council

Pollock Nittany Residence Association

South Halls Residence Association

Undergraduate Student Government

West Halls Residence Association

University Affiliate

Distinguished Speaker Series

Lion Ambassadors

Senior Class Gift Committee

University Concert Committee

University Park Allocation Committee

The Best & Worst

The Ten BEST Things About Penn State

1	Academics balanced with partying
2	School spirit and Nittany Lion pride
3	Joe Paterno and Penn State football
4	The beautiful central PA landscape
5	THON
6	Homecoming
7	Campus safety
8	Huge alumni presence nationwide
9	Local atmosphere
10	Wide range of student activities

The Ten WORST Things About Penn State

1 Rural location (isolation)

2 Alcohol-centered culture

3 Lack of parking

4 Lack of diversity

5 Lack of organized nightlife and clubs

6 Big, bad winter weather

7 Repetitive campus food

8 Tiny rooms in East Halls

9 Crowded football weekends

10 Constant tuition increases

Visiting

The Lowdown On...
Visiting

Hotel Information:

On-Campus Hotels

The Nittany Lion Inn
200 W. Park Ave.
State College, PA 16803
(814) 865-8500
Fax: (814) 865-8501
Distance from Campus:
Less than 1 mile
Price Range: $90–$109

The Penn Stater
215 Innovation Blvd.
State College, PA 16803
(814) 863-5000
Fax: (814) 865-8501
Distance from Campus:
Less than 1 mile
Price Range: $90–$120

➜

Area Hotels

Atherton Hotel
125 S. Atherton St.
State College, PA 16801
(814) 231-2100
Distance from Campus:
About 1.5 miles
Price Range: $79–$119

Courtyard by Marriott
1730 University Dr.
State College, PA 16801
(814) 238-1861
Distance from Campus:
About 1.5 miles
Price Range: $89–209

Days Inn–Penn State
240 S. Pugh St.
State College, PA 16801
(814) 238-8454
Distance from Campus:
Less than 1 mile
Price Range: $67–$90

Hilton Garden Inn
1221 E. College Ave.
State College, PA 16801
(814) 272-1221
Distance from Campus:
About 2 miles
Price Range: $90–$119

Ramada Inn
1450 S. Atherton St.
State College, PA 16801
(814) 238-3001
Distance from Campus:
About 2 miles
Price Range: $55–$80

Residence Inn by Marriott
1555 University Dr.
State College, PA 16801
(814) 235-6960
Distance from Campus:
About 2 miles
Price Range: $104–$135

Take a Campus Virtual Tour

www.alumni.psu.edu/VRPennState/VirtualAmbassador

To Schedule a Group Information Session or Interview

www.psu.edu/dept/admissions/visits/visitup

Contact the Office of Admissions; the easiest way is to log onto the Web site, as it provides a full University calendar and allows you to register. For help or any other information, contact the Admissions Office in 201 Shields Building at (814) 865-5471.

Penn State typically does not require an interview for its prospective students. A visitation will include a campus tour and group information session. After that, it is your responsibility to make contact with the departments of your choice to schedule appointments with an advisor.

Visiting a Particular College

Contact the advising center of each college to arrange individual visits or find out about open houses. At Penn State, visits to particular colleges will only be scheduled on weekdays.

Advising Center
116 Arts Building
(814) 865-9523

Aerospace
233 Hammond Building
(814) 865-2569

Agricultural & Biological
249 Agricultural Engineering Building
(814) 865-7792

Architectural Engineering
225 Engineering, Unit A
(814) 863-2078

Architecture
206 Engineering, Unit C
(814) 865-9535

Bioengineering
233 Hallowell
(814) 865-1407

Chemical
158 Fenske Lab
(814) 865-2574

Civil and Environmental
218 Sackett Building
(814) 863-3087

College of Agricultural
Sciences Advising Center
101 Agricultural
Administration Building
(814) 865-7521

College of Communications
Advising Center
204 Carnegie Building
(814) 865-1503

College of Earth and
Mineral Sciences
Advising Center
25 Deike Building
(814) 863-2751

College of Education
Advising Center
228 Chambers Building
(814) 863-0488

College of Engineering
Advising Center
208 Hammond Building
(814) 863-3064

College of Human
Health and Development
Advising Center
215 Hendricks Building
(814) 865-2156

College of Liberal Arts
Advising Center
136 Sparks Building
(814) 865-2545

Computer Science and
Engineering
220 Pond Lab
(814) 865-9505

Division of Undergraduate
Studies (Undecided Students)
Advising Center
118 Grange Building
(814) 865-7576

Eberly College of Science
Advising Center
213 Whitmore Lab
(814) 863-0284

Electrical
121 Electrical Engineering
(EE) East
(814) 865-7272

Industrial
10 Leonhard Building
(814) 865-7601

Integrative Arts
215 Wagner Building
(814) 865-1750

Landscape Architecture
210 Engineering, Unit D
(814) 865-9511

Mechanical and Nuclear
138 Reber Building
(814) 863-1503

Music
233 Music Building
(814) 863-0418

School of Information
Sciences and Technology
Advising Center
006 Thomas building
(814) 865-8947

The Smeal College Of
Business Administration
Advising Center
104 Beam Building
(814) 863-1947

Theater
103 Arts Building
(814) 865-7586

Visual Arts
103 Arts Building
(814) 865-0444

Directions to Campus

From Pittsburgh (138 miles, 2.5–3 hours)
- Take Route 22 east to I-99 North (Altoona).
- Take I-99 to Route 220, then Route 322 East (Bald Eagle).
- Follow Route 322 East to State College.
- From Route 322, take the Penn State University/Innovation Park exit and, follow the local area directions (pg 162).

From Washington D.C. (188 miles, 4–5 hours)
- Take I-95 North or the Baltimore-Washington Parkway to West Loop I-695 to I-83 North.
- Continue on I-83 North to the I-81 interchange.
- Follow I-81 South to Route 322/22 West.
- Proceed west on Route 322 to State College.
- Take the exit at the Penn State University/Innovation Park exit and follow the local area directions (pg 162).

From Northern New Jersey (234 miles from New York City, 4.5–5 hours)
- I-80 West in PA to exit 161 (Bellefonte).
- Follow PA 26 South to US 220 South.
- Take exit 74 for Innovation Park/Penn State University and follow the local area directions (pg 162).

From Philadelphia (195 miles, 4–4.5 hours)
- Take the Schuylkill Expressway to the PA Turnpike.
- Leave the Turnpike at exit 247 (Harrisburg East-formerly exit 19).
- Follow I-283 North to I-83.
- Proceed north on I-83 to the I-81 interchange.
- Follow I-81 South to Route 322/22 West.
- Proceed West on Route 322 to State College.
- Take exit 74 at the Penn State University/Innovation Park exit and follow the local area directions (pg 162).

From Western Pennsylvania and Ohio (5 hours from the Ohio/Pennsylvania border)

- Take I-80 East to exit 161 (formerly exit 24).
- Take Route 26 South.
- Follow Route 26 South to US 220 South.
- From Route 220, take the Penn State University/Innovation Park exit and follow the local area directions below.

Local Area Directions (From the Penn State University/ Innovation Park exit on 322)

- Take Route 322 to the Penn State University/Innovation Park exit.
- If you are traveling on Route 322 westbound, you will approach a traffic light at the end of the exit ramp; turn right onto Park Avenue toward campus, and away from Innovation Park.
- If you are traveling on Route 322 eastbound, make a right at the end of the exit ramp and proceed onto Park Avenue toward campus, and away from Innovation Park.
- At the fourth traffic light on Park Avenue, turn left onto University Drive.
- Go to the first traffic light and turn right onto Curtin Road.
- The Shields Building parking lot (Orange E) is the first left after you turn onto Curtin Road.

Words to Know

Academic Probation – A suspension imposed on a student if he or she fails to keep up with the school's minimum academic requirements. Those unable to improve their grades after receiving this warning can face dismissal.

Beer Pong/Beirut – A drinking game involving cups of beer arranged in a pyramid shape on each side of a table. The goal is to get a ping pong ball into one of the opponent's cups by throwing the ball or hitting it with a paddle. If the ball lands in a cup, the opponent is required to drink the beer.

Bid – An invitation from a fraternity or sorority to 'pledge' (join) that specific house.

Blue-Light Phone – Brightly-colored phone posts with a blue light bulb on top. These phones exist for security purposes and are located at various outside locations around most campuses. In an emergency, a student can pick up one of these phones (free of charge) to connect with campus police or a security escort.

Campus Police – Police who are specifically assigned to a given institution. Campus police are typically not regular city officers; they are employed by the university in a full-time capacity.

Club Sports – A level of sports that falls somewhere between varsity and intramural. If a student is unable to commit to a varsity team but has a lot of passion for athletics, a club sport could be a better, less intense option. Even less demanding, intramural (IM) sports often involve no traveling and considerably less time.

Cocaine – An illegal drug. Also known as "coke" or "blow," cocaine often resembles a white crystalline or powdery substance. It is highly addictive and dangerous.

Common Application – An application with which students can apply to multiple schools.

Course Registration – The period of official class selection for the upcoming quarter or semester. Prior to registration, it is best to prepare several back-up courses in case a particular class becomes full. If a course is full, students can place themselves on the waitlist, although this still does not guarantee entry.

Division Athletics – Athletic classifications range from Division I to Division III. Division IA is the most competitive, while Division III is considered to be the least competitive.

Dorm – A dorm (or dormitory) is an on-campus housing facility. Dorms can provide a range of options from suite-style rooms to more communal options that include shared bathrooms. Most first-year students live in dorms. Some upperclassmen who wish to stay on campus also choose this option.

Early Action – An application option with which a student can apply to a school and receive an early acceptance response without a binding commitment. This system is becoming less and less available.

Early Decision – An application option that students should use only if they are certain they plan to attend the school in question. If a student applies using the early decision option and is admitted, he or she is required and bound to attend that university. Admission rates are usually higher among students who apply through early decision, as the student is clearly indicating that the school is his or her first choice.

Ecstasy – An illegal drug. Also known as "E" or "X," ecstasy looks like a pill and most resembles an aspirin. Considered a party drug, ecstasy is very dangerous and can be deadly.

Ethernet – An extremely fast Internet connection available in most university-owned residence halls. To use an Ethernet connection properly, a student will need a network card and cable for his or her computer.

Fake ID – A counterfeit identification card that contains false information. Most commonly, students get fake IDs with altered birthdates so that they appear to be older than 21 (and therefore of legal drinking age). Even though it is illegal, many college students have fake IDs in hopes of purchasing alcohol or getting into bars.

Frosh – Slang for "freshman" or "freshmen."

Hazing – Initiation rituals administered by some fraternities or sororities as part of the pledging process. Many universities have outlawed hazing due to its degrading, and sometimes dangerous, nature.

Intramurals (IMs) – A popular, and usually free, sport league in which students create teams and compete against one another. These sports vary in competitiveness and can include a range of activities—everything from billiards to water polo. IM sports are a great way to meet people with similar interests.

Keg – Officially called a half-barrel, a keg contains roughly 200 12-ounce servings of beer.

LSD – An illegal drug, also known as acid, this hallucinogenic drug most commonly resembles a tab of paper.

Marijuana – An illegal drug, also known as weed or pot; along with alcohol, marijuana is one of the most commonly-found drugs on campuses across the country.

Major –The focal point of a student's college studies; a specific topic that is studied for a degree. Examples of majors include physics, English, history, computer science, economics, business, and music. Many students decide on a specific major before arriving on campus, while others are simply "undecided" until declaring a major. Those who are extremely interested in two areas can also choose to double major.

Meal Block – The equivalent of one meal. Students on a meal plan usually receive a fixed number of meals per week. Each meal, or "block," can be redeemed at the school's dining facilities in place of cash. Often, a student's weekly allotment of meal blocks will be forfeited if not used.

Minor – An additional focal point in a student's education. Often serving as a complement or addition to a student's main area of focus, a minor has fewer requirements and prerequisites to fulfill than a major. Minors are not required for graduation from most schools; however some students who want to explore many different interests choose to pursue both a major and a minor.

Mushrooms – An illegal drug. Also known as "'shrooms," this drug resembles regular mushrooms but is extremely hallucinogenic.

Off-Campus Housing – Housing from a particular landlord or rental group that is not affiliated with the university. Depending on the college, off-campus housing can range from extremely popular to non-existent. Students who choose to live off campus are typically given more freedom, but they also have to deal with possible subletting scenarios, furniture, bills, and other issues. In addition to these factors, rental prices and distance often affect a student's decision to move off campus.

Office Hours – Time that teachers set aside for students who have questions about coursework. Office hours are a good forum for students to go over any problems and to show interest in the subject material.

Pledging – The early phase of joining a fraternity or sorority, pledging takes place after a student has gone through rush and received a bid. Pledging usually lasts between one and two semesters. Once the pledging period is complete and a particular student has done everything that is required to become a member, that student is considered a brother or sister. If a fraternity or a sorority would decide to "haze" a group of students, this initiation would take place during the pledging period.

Private Institution – A school that does not use tax revenue to subsidize education costs. Private schools typically cost more than public schools and are usually smaller.

Prof – Slang for "professor."

Public Institution – A school that uses tax revenue to subsidize education costs. Public schools are often a good value for in-state residents and tend to be larger than most private colleges.

Quarter System (or Trimester System) – A type of academic calendar system. In this setup, students take classes for three academic periods. The first quarter usually starts in late September or early October and concludes right before Christmas. The second quarter usually starts around early to mid–January and finishes up around March or April. The last academic quarter, or "third quarter," usually starts in late March or early April and finishes up in late May or Mid-June. The fourth quarter is summer. The major difference between the quarter system and semester system is that students take more, less comprehensive courses under the quarter calendar.

RA (Resident Assistant) – A student leader who is assigned to a particular floor in a dormitory in order to help to the other students who live there. An RA's duties include ensuring student safety and providing assistance wherever possible.

Recitation – An extension of a specific course; a review session. Some classes, particularly large lectures, are supplemented with mandatory recitation sessions that provide a relatively personal class setting.

Rolling Admissions – A form of admissions. Most commonly found at public institutions, schools with this type of policy continue to accept students throughout the year until their class sizes are met. For example, some schools begin accepting students as early as December and will continue to do so until April or May.

Room and Board – This figure is typically the combined cost of a university-owned room and a meal plan.

Room Draw/Housing Lottery – A common way to pick on-campus room assignments for the following year. If a student decides to remain in university-owned housing, he or she is assigned a unique number that, along with seniority, is used to determine his or her housing for the next year.

Rush – The period in which students can meet the brothers and sisters of a particular chapter and find out if a given fraternity or sorority is right for them. Rushing a fraternity or a sorority is not a requirement at any school. The goal of rush is to give students who are serious about pledging a feel for what to expect.

Semester System – The most common type of academic calendar system at college campuses. This setup typically includes two semesters in a given school year. The fall semester starts around the end of August or early September and concludes before winter vacation. The spring semester usually starts in mid-January and ends in late April or May.

Student Center/Rec Center/Student Union – A common area on campus that often contains study areas, recreation facilities, and eateries. This building is often a good place to meet up with fellow students; depending on the school, the student center can have a huge role or a non-existent role in campus life.

Student ID – A university-issued photo ID that serves as a student's key to school-related functions. Some schools require students to show these cards in order to get into dorms, libraries, cafeterias, and other facilities. In addition to storing meal plan information, in some cases, a student ID can actually work as a debit card and allow students to purchase things from bookstores or local shops.

Suite – A type of dorm room. Unlike dorms that feature communal bathrooms shared by the entire floor, suites offer bathrooms shared only among the suite. Suite-style dorm rooms can house anywhere from two to ten students.

TA (Teacher's Assistant) – An undergraduate or grad student who helps in some manner with a specific course. In some cases, a TA will teach a class, assist a professor, grade assignments, or conduct office hours.

Undergraduate – A student in the process of studying for his or her bachelor's degree.

California Colleges

California dreamin'?
This book is a must have for you!

CALIFORNIA COLLEGES
7¼" X 10", 762 Pages Paperback
$29.95 Retail
1-59658-501-3

Stanford, UC Berkeley, Caltech—California is home
to some of America's greatest institutes of higher
learning. *California Colleges* gives the lowdown on 24
of the best, side by side, in one prodigious volume.

New England Colleges

Looking for peace in the Northeast?
Pick up this regional guide to New England!

NEW ENGLAND COLLEGES
7¼" X 10", 1015 Pages Paperback
$29.95 Retail
1-59658-504-8

New England is the birthplace of many prestigious universities, and with so many to choose from, picking the right school can be a tough decision. With inside information on over 34 competive Northeastern schools, *New England Colleges* provides the same high-quality information prospective students expect from College Prowler in one all-inclusive, easy-to-use reference.

Schools of the South

Headin' down south? This book will help you find your way to the perfect school!

SCHOOLS OF THE SOUTH
7¼" X 10", 773 Pages Paperback
$29.95 Retail
1-59658-503-X

Southern pride is always strong. Whether it's across town or across state, many Southern students are devoted to their home sweet home. *Schools of the South* offers an honest student perspective on 36 universities available south of the Mason-Dixon.

Untangling
the Ivy League

The ultimate book for everything Ivy!

UNTANGLING THE IVY LEAGUE
7¼" X 10", 567 Pages Paperback
$24.95 Retail
1-59658-500-5

Ivy League students, alumni, admissions officers,
and other top insiders get together to tell it like it is.
Untangling the Ivy League covers every aspect—from
admissions and athletics to secret societies and urban
legends—of the nation's eight oldest, wealthiest, and
most competitive colleges and universities.

Need Help Paying For School?

Apply for our scholarship!

College Prowler awards thousands of dollars a year to students who compose the best essays. E-mail scholarship@collegeprowler.com for more information, or call 1-800-290-2682.

Apply now at **www.collegeprowler.com**

Tell Us What Life Is Really Like at Your School!

Have you ever wanted to let people know what your college is really like? Now's your chance to help millions of high school students choose the right college.

Let your voice be heard.

Check out **www.collegeprowler.com** for more info!

Need More Help?

Do you have more questions about this school? Can't find a certain statistic? College Prowler is here to help. We are the best source of college information out there. We have a network of thousands of students who can get the latest information on any school to you ASAP. E-mail us at info@collegeprowler.com with your college-related questions.

E-Mail Us Your College-Related Questions!

Check out *www.collegeprowler.com* for more details.
1-800-290-2682

Write For Us!

Get published! Voice your opinion.

Writing a College Prowler guidebook is both fun and rewarding; our open-ended format allows your own creativity free reign. Our writers have been featured in national newspapers and have seen their names in bookstores across the country. Now is your chance to break into the publishing industry with one of the country's fastest-growing publishers!

Apply now at ***www.collegeprowler.com***

Contact editor@collegeprowler.com or call 1-800-290-2682 for more details.

Pros and Cons

Still can't figure out if this is the right school for you?
You've already read through this in-depth guide; why not
list the pros and cons? It will really help with narrowing down
your decision and determining whether or not
this school is right for you.

Pros	Cons
....	....
....	....
....	....
....	....
....	....
....	....
....	....
....	....
....	....
....	....
....	....
....	....
....	....

Pros and Cons

Still can't figure out if this is the right school for you?
You've already read through this in-depth guide; why not
list the pros and cons? It will really help with narrowing down
your decision and determining whether or not
this school is right for you.

Pros	Cons
....	....
....	....
....	....
....	....
....	....
....	....
....	....
....	....
....	....
....	....
....	....
....	....
....	....

Notes

....

....

....

....

....

....

....

....

....

....

....

....

....

Notes